TIM
RICHMOND

THE FAST LIFE AND REMARKABLE TIMES
OF NASCAR'S TOP GUN

DAVID POOLE

www.SportsPublishingLLC.com

ISBN: 1-58261-833-X

© 2005 by David Poole

Publisher: Peter L. Bannon and Joseph J. Bannon Sr.
Senior managing editor: Susan M. Moyer
Acquisitions and developmental editor: Lynnette A. Bogard
Art director: K. Jeffrey Higgerson
Book design: Jennifer L. Polson
Dust jacket photo insert design: Heidi Norsen
Photo editor: Erin Linden-Levy
Vice president of sales and marketing: Kevin King
Media and promotions managers: Kelley Brown (regional),
    Randy Fouts (national), Maurey Williamson (print)

Printed in the United States

Sports Publishing L.L.C.
804 North Neil Street
Champaign, IL 61820

Phone: 1-877-424-2665
Fax: 217-363-2073
Web site: www.SportsPublishingLLC.com

For the race fans
who remember Tim Richmond

... and the ones
who never got to see him race

CONTENTS

ACKNOWLEDGMENTS vi

CHAPTER 1 1

CHAPTER 2 7

CHAPTER 3 19

CHAPTER 4 27

CHAPTER 5 35

CHAPTER 6 43

CHAPTER 7 55

CHAPTER 8 67

CHAPTER 9 79

CHAPTER 10 91

CHAPTER 11 103

CHAPTER 12 111

CHAPTER 13 121

CHAPTER 14 131

CHAPTER 15 141

CHAPTER 16 151

CHAPTER 17 161

CHAPTER 18 173

CHAPTER 19 183

ACKNOWLEDGMENTS

The idea of writing a book about Tim Richmond should have been obvious.

Anyone who has been around NASCAR for any length of time knows people who believe Richmond was a singular talent and a man who lived an extraordinary life that had an extraordinarily tragic end.

However, the thought of doing this book never really hit me until I sat beside longtime Charlotte television broadcaster Harold Johnson on a flight back from a Carolina Panthers NFL playoff game in St. Louis in January 2004. Johnson reminisced about how much he enjoyed watching Richmond race and we wondered aloud why no one had ever written a book that covered his life and career.

The more I thought about that conversation, the more I wanted to try it.

With the encouragement and support of Lynnette Bogard of Sports Publishing LLC, for whom I'd written a book of NASCAR stories with driving legend Buddy Baker, I began the initial research. Within a matter of days, two things became apparent. First, I absolutely wanted to try to tell this story. Second, I knew I would never be able to do it right without the help of Tim's family.

Sandy Welsh, Tim's half-sister, was understandably leery of cooperating with a stranger who tracked her down in Mooresville to ask if he could write about the good times and the bad times her family had gone through. There have been times when stories in the newspaper for which I have covered NASCAR since 1997, *The Charlotte Observer*, caused Welsh great pain. I am certain that there are things in this book that she would just as soon not see in print again. What I promised when I began working on this book was to write as accurately as I could about how Tim lived, not just about how he died. I fervently hope that when she reads the finished product, she will believe I kept that promise. Either way, this book would not have been possible without her cooperation and her spirit. I am deeply grateful.

Many of Richmond's friends from NASCAR and throughout the racing world sat down and talked about a man they all have a remarkable lasting fondness for. Barry Dodson, Fred Miller, Dr. Jerry Punch, Harold Elliott, Kyle Petty, Rick Hendrick, Jimmy Johnson, Bob Tezak, Tim Brewer and Raymond Beadle were gracious with their time and their memories. Dr. David Dodson, Geoffrey Bodine, Barry Slotnick, Dale Inman and Chip Williams provided details that helped tell the story. Dr. Punch and Dr. Dodson helped me try to put AIDS in the proper context of the time in which Richmond was diagnosed. Donald Davidson of Indianapolis Motor Speedway helped guide me through Richmond's experiences at America's most famous race track. I am grateful to each of these people as well as to many others in the sport who spoke on background and helped me understand the era when the events in this book took place.

The staff of *NASCAR Scene* could not have been more helpful in allowing me to use their archives to verify details of races during Richmond's NASCAR career. I also used stories from the archives of *The Charlotte Observer* and other publications to verify details of those events and contemporary quotations describing them. In instances in the book where quotations are given without direct attribution to a source, those remarks appeared in several publications immediately following the events they refer to.

The work of Tom Higgins, who covered NASCAR at *The Observer* before I did, and Tom Sorensen, a columnist and current colleague at that newspaper, were particularly valuable. Liz Clarke, a former *Observer* colleague who now works with the *Washington Post*, wrote a marvelous story on the 10th anniversary of Richmond's death that proved particularly beneficial in leading me to people who could talk in detail about events in this book. I am also grateful to my boss, Mike Persinger, for allowing me to find the time to assemble information and write these words during the course of a busy racing season.

I also want to thank Alan Boodman, whose Internet site www.racing-reference.com provided a remarkably useful data base through which details of Richmond's career could be verified. For a statistics nut like myself, his site is a gold mine.

Above all else, I thank my wife, Katy, for putting up with me while I was working on this book. Along with friends and colleagues on the racing beat, Katy listened to me retell the stories I was learning about Richmond. She seemed to understand that sometimes, I just had to share them to get them out of my head. But then again, she has to be a very understanding woman—she is, after all, married to me. As is the case with everything I do, she's a big part of this effort. And I love her with all of my heart.

CHAPTER 1

On a Sunday morning in July, hours before the 1989 AC Spark Plug 500 at Pocono Raceway where one of NASCAR Winston Cup racing's most meteoric careers began nine years earlier, Dr. Jerry Punch was looking for Barry Dodson.

Punch was a pit reporter preparing for ESPN's telecast while Dodson, a crew chief in stock-car racing's top series, was readying the No. 27 Pontiac that Rusty Wallace would drive that day for Blue Max Racing. It was not unusual for the two to chat in the hours before a race, since Punch reported from various teams' pits and needed to know about last-minute changes made by Dodson, whose team's car was starting sixth and figured to contend for the win.

But Punch had more than that day's race on his mind. Being a pit reporter was a part-time occupation for Punch—he was also an emergency room doctor, and through that profession he sometimes knew more about the men he covered than he could allow himself to say on the air.

This was one of those times.

At the same time, special preparations were also underway in a hospital room more than 1,200 miles away. The staff at Good Samaritan Hospital in West Palm Beach, Florida, set up a television near the bed where a 34-year-old patient was fighting the ravages of a disease the medical community was just beginning to understand. The nurses and staff knew Tim Richmond's name, and some knew what he had done for a living before he got sick. But few of them knew fully just how good Richmond had been at his job, that he did it in a way that made people who saw him do it—and some who did it with him—marvel at his prowess.

Punch and the ESPN crew hoped to change that by showing the people in that hospital room—as well as stock car racing fans all across the country looking in that afternoon—just how accomplished Richmond had been as a driver in America's most popular form of motorsports.

As Dodson worked on the No. 27 Pontiac in the garage, running down the kind of checklist every NASCAR crew chief goes through on the morning of a race, he noticed Punch walking over. "When I come up to talk to you early in the race today," Punch said, "you should say something about Tim."

Dodson's heart jumped into his throat.

It had been months since virtually anyone in the NASCAR garage had seen or heard from Richmond. But Dodson knew Punch's connections meant the man everyone called "Doc" knew as much as anybody about how Richmond was really doing. "Jerry was the first guy to tell me that Tim was sick," Dodson said. "Like everybody else, I heard he had pneumonia. When Tim got worse, all Jerry would say is that Tim wasn't getting any better. But he never did tell me anything beyond the fact that Tim was just very sick."

So Dodson took to heart Punch's request to say something about the driver who'd helped Dodson and Blue Max Racing lay the foundation on which Wallace was building a run toward the 1989 championship.

As the start of the Pocono race approached, people began gathering in Richmond's hospital room. That, too, was nothing unusual. All his life, Richmond never had a problem drawing a crowd. He thrived on approval and affection the way a plant feeds on sunshine and water, and his good looks and happy-go-lucky demeanor helped him get it.

By that day, however, Richmond was losing his battle against a cruel, heartless disease that had struck him less than three years earlier, just as the hotshot hot-rodder from the country's heartland finally had the Southern-fried sport of stock car racing by the tail. By July 1989 Richmond, who once could barely stand to be alone, had cut himself off from everyone except for his doting mother and immediate family.

It had been nearly a year and a half since many of his friends in racing had talked to him, but that didn't mean people in NASCAR weren't talking about him. Gossip filled the void left by the absence of any real knowledge in the racing world's most mobile small town—the traveling NASCAR "family" that moves each week from track to track across the country, and the rumors about Richmond were rampant.

His days as the life of the NASCAR party had finally caught up with him, people said. Drugs had ravaged his body, they said. Some even said Richmond had AIDS, acquired immune deficiency syndrome, a death sentence that at that time in American culture carried a social stigma that could indelibly stain a lifetime of accomplishments.

Dodson had heard all of the rumors but refused to listen. All he knew was what "Doc" Punch had told him—that Richmond was very, very sick. Dodson was almost too busy running Wallace's team now to think about how much he missed Richmond. But he knew that Richmond had helped the team earn its way to victory lane with a talent that was so strong it challenged Blue Max to build cars good enough to keep up with him. Without Richmond, the success Wallace and Dodson were enjoying in 1989 would have not been possible. No matter what anybody said about Richmond, Dodson would never forget that.

Dodson's memories of Richmond were especially strong at Pocono, a venue Richmond loved and a place where he'd flourished since his very first race in a stock car there in 1980.

It was there in 1983 where Richmond won for the first time on a non-road course NASCAR track. Richmond won again at Pocono in June of 1986, snapping a 64-race winless streak that had been torturous for a driver who loved winning almost as much as he loved the applause that came with it. That victory was also Richmond's first for an up-and-coming car owner named Rick Hendrick and for crew chief Harry Hyde, a veteran of the stock car racing wars who was trying to prove wrong those who believed the sport had passed him by. It also was a big part of something even bigger, a streak of success for Richmond that finally confirmed what many in the sport believed all along—that with the right people, the right equipment and the right focus, this driver with seemingly boundless talent was destined to take his place among the sport's greatest ever.

Three races later in 1986, the NASCAR schedule brought Richmond, Hyde and their No. 25 Chevrolet back to Pocono for a victory that years later would prove to be tough for even movie critics to swallow. A driver wrecks and finds his car damaged so badly it won't drive forward? He whirls it around and backs it around the track and into his pit? His crew makes quick repairs and the driver roars back onto the track, winning the race by an eyelash at the checkered flag? Yeah, right.

But it happened, and as crazy as it was—with a finish that left Richmond and another driver wondering which one of them should go to victory lane—what happened at Pocono in June the next year seemed even more impossible. No driver in what was already emerging as the world's most competitive form of motorsports could miss three months, and then win in his first full race back after nearly dying. Not even Tim Richmond could do that, not even at Pocono. But he did.

So in July 1989, ESPN planned to send a get-well card from a race track in Pennsylvania to a hospital room in south Florida. When Punch put the microphone in front of him, Dodson dedicated the No. 27 Pontiac's efforts that day to his former driver and his friend. "Our run today is for you, Tim," Dodson said. "You own this place, you own Pocono. I hope you're feeling better."

It was still early in the race, in which Wallace would finish second behind Bill Elliott. Tape rolled showing Richmond's unbelievable Pocono victory from three years earlier—the 1986 July victory in which he'd backed his crippled car to pit road and then rallied from more than a lap down to win in a dramatic, last-lap battle to the checkered flag. The highlights ended with a raucous victory lane, with Richmond, Hyde, Hendrick and their team spraying beer and champagne all over each other. In those moments, they were the hottest team in NASCAR and their driver, the handsome hero whose popularity with the fans was growing with every success, was leading the celebration.

"Tim had Hollywood good looks and the charisma of a Tom Cruise," Punch said. "There he was in victory lane with the team all around him and beauty queens hanging all over him. It was important for the people at the hospital to see Tim the way he really was, when he was healthy and handsome and vital, and not like the way he was as they saw him every day at the hospital."

As the highlights played, fans around America got one more look at a man who had been born 20 years too late and, at the same time, 20 years too early to fit comfortably into his sport. As the 1989 season headed through the summer, other stories were emerging.

Richmond was out of sight, and he was beginning to slip out of mind. That was just fine with some people within the sport's hierarchy.

Within just a few weeks, Tim Richmond's name would make the headlines one last time, and some of the questions would be answered. Many others never will.

But on that Sunday, if only for a few minutes, ESPN viewers saw just what NASCAR had lost when fate cut short what could have been one of the most colorful and storied careers any stock-car driver has ever enjoyed. In that hospital room in Florida, doctors and nurses could see how the man they tried to help as much as they could every day had once been so full of life. And the patient got to remember the good times. Tim Richmond's eyesight was no longer as good as it had been, but in that moment, the old fire danced again in his eyes.

"Tim wasn't afraid of dying," Barry Dodson said years later in remembering his friend. "He was afraid of never having lived."

In that regard, Richmond never had a thing to worry about.

CHAPTER 2

Timothy Lee Richmond's competitive fire burned almost from the day he was born, on June 7, 1955, in Ashland, Ohio.

Before agreeing to fetch the mail each day, young Tim insisted that his father, Al, put a stopwatch on him as he ran to the roadside mailbox at the family's house just south of Ashland, about 65 miles south of Cleveland.

"He was just a little thing," said his half-sister, Sandy Welsh. "Every day, he'd want to know if he had beat his test time."

Evelyn Warner divorced her first husband soon after Sandy was born in 1940. She met Al Richmond through their jobs with pipeline construction companies—Al was a welder and Evelyn was a field-office manager. Both traveled extensively and they dated for several years before getting married.

Al Richmond had little formal education, but he did have a keen intelligence for seeing how things worked—or should work. It was a trait he'd pass on to his son. As the United States economy roared to life following World War II, construction boomed. When Al watched crews gash open highways so pipes could be run across them, he knew there had to be a better way. Al went to work designing a machine to bore underneath the roadways. He sold the farm, and the family moved to Newark, Ohio, where he rented an abandoned gas station and built his first boring machine. "He took it out, sold it, then he came back and built another one," Welsh said.

From those beginnings, Richmond Manufacturing grew. The family moved back to Ashland and Al bought land on Route 42 east of town that had an old house and a Quonset hut on it. It would eventually become the home base to a thriving enterprise. "Eventually they sold his machines all over the world," Welsh said. Al built machines that tunneled pathways through which pipes from two to 60 inches in diameter could pass. "He later designed a coal recovery machine to go into the mines after they were finished and bring out what was left. He had patents on all of that stuff. He didn't have a high school diploma. But he was sharp as a tack. You could give him anything with math and he could just sit right there and click it off. He came up with the ideas and then went and got them built."

Office work, however, was another matter.

"Al hated paper," Welsh said. "People shuffling it around in an office seemed like such a waste of time and money to Al." That was where Evelyn came in. "Al and mother were such a good mix," Welsh said. "She had the business savvy. She handled the purse strings."

Tim, meanwhile, was doing more than running around the family's land on foot. While he was still a toddler, Al bought him a go-kart that the youngster drove on the driveways and paths around the house—and sometimes even across the factory floor at Richmond Manufacturing.

"He kept that go-kart it in this little barn we had," Welsh remembered. "The barn floor was raised up a little bit, a couple of inches, from the ground and one day he came flying through there and the wheels of the go-kart hit that ledge. Tim bit the tip of his tongue so hard that he had to get stitches in it."

By the time he was eight, Tim turned his attention to quarter horses. He showed them for much of the next decade, winning ribbons, trophies and elaborate saddles that Evelyn kept—along with virtually everything else her son ever drew, wrote or received.

Tim was not a particularly stellar student. Years later, he would say that he doubted that he ever read more than a handful of books in his life. But if he was interested in something, he could learn it rapidly by watching someone else do it. Nobody, for instance, ever had to teach him how to drive a car on the street. "I just watched my parents drive and picked it up," Richmond said.

The same process applied to flying an airplane. Al flew a company-owned plane on business, with Tim often accompanying him on those trips. Tim watched and learned, and by the age of 14 he had soloed in a plane Al kept at the county airport near Ashland.

Tim was a good athlete but was not at all happy attending public schools in Ohio. He was seen as a rich kid, and that sometimes led to conflicts with some of his classmates who grew up on the farms surrounding the town.

"They had some stabbings and that kind of thing, and this was out in the cornfields," Richmond would say in a 1985 interview in *NASCAR Grand National Scene* magazine. "It was as bad as New York City." With the family's business thriving, the search for a private school for Tim led to the Miami Military Academy in Florida. Evelyn, who by that point had developed a profound closeness to her only son that would grow deeper as the years went on, found a condominium in nearby Fort Lauderdale. While Welsh stayed in Ohio and helped Al run the business, Evelyn spent much of her time near Tim after he enrolled in the academy.

"I thought the weather might be nice down there," Richmond said. "When I got there, I thought it was a major mistake at first. But it turned out to be pretty good."

By the end of his four-year stay, Richmond might have been his company's commander. But that meant he would have to get up early each morning and balance the time commitments required for officer's training with football practice. He was late for the first two days of officer's training, and was demoted.

"By the time I got out of school, I was a first sergeant," Richmond said. "I went backward." Richmond didn't really want to be anybody's boss. As a high-ranking officer, it would have been his job to tell his classmates what they needed to do and to mete out discipline when they failed to comply. By the time he got himself busted back to sergeant, all he had to be sure of was that everybody was present and accounted for and that the lights were turned off at night and back on in the morning. That much he could deal with.

Richmond had no problem, however, standing out athletically. He played football and ran track and excelled at both. The Miami Military Academy Eagles ran a single-wing offense, a system where the football can be snapped to any one of several players in the backfield on any play. Richmond, wearing jersey No. 13, frequently displayed the kind of versatility required of a back in that system. In his senior season, the Eagles played Dade Christian and won 40-20 to snap their opponent's 17-game winning streak. Richmond threw touchdown passes of 17 and five yards that day. He also ran for another score on an eight-yard run. He had a 10-yard touchdown reception on a double-reverse pass. He also returned a kickoff 85 yards for yet another touchdown and scored on a pair of two-point conversions, meaning he had a hand in 34 of his team's 40 points. In that same game, he also intercepted a pass and caused a fumble while playing on defense.

When he went back to Ohio during the summers between the school years, the financial success his father's business was enjoying helped provide Tim with plenty of toys to play with. For his 16th birthday, he got a brand new Pontiac Trans-Am. Later his parents bought him a Corvette.

Fred Miller lived in Mansfield, Ohio, and was one of a group of teenagers who hung around at a custom paint shop owned by one the area's former racers.

"I went in there one night and there was this brand new Corvette parked there," Miller said. "It had a high-rise manifold and everything else you could think of on it. It was getting a custom paint job." Miller asked who owned the car and was told a young kid from Ashland named Tim Richmond had brought it in.

"A couple of days later I was back down there and Tim was there," Miller said. "We started talking and he told me about his whole situation, that he was going to military school and all of that." That meeting was the start of a lifelong friendship between Miller and Richmond, and it wasn't long before Miller would get a taste of what adventures might follow for him and his new pal.

"We were just sitting around one day and Tim said, 'You want to go for an airplane ride?'" Miller said. "I don't think I had ever been in an airplane in my life, but I was young and I said, 'Sure.' So we hopped in the car and drove out to the airport there in Ashland to the hangar. He rolls up the door and there is this little Piper Cub or something sitting there. We climb in and sit down and he reaches over and pulls out this manual.

"What are you doing?" Miller said.

"Just refreshing my memory," Richmond said.

"Jesus," Miller said in looking back on that day. "How stupid was I not to get out right then?"

When Miller and Richmond weren't hanging around at the paint shop, they could be found in Ashland where another local racer kept a car that performed wheel stands between rounds of competition at drag races. Miller began tagging along and eventually got a job working for a drag-racing star named Raymond Beadle.

Richmond, meanwhile, enrolled in college in Ashland but lasted about a year before going to work in the family business. Sometimes he was the company pilot and, at least in theory, he also was a sales manager. "Most of the time he'd lock his office door and sleep," Sandy Welsh said. "He'd take the machines out and put them to work, but that wasn't who he wanted to be."

Since his contributions were hardly critical to the overall success of the family business, Richmond had plenty of time to develop his own growing connections to racing. Had he been living in the South, he most likely would have started going to a dirt track and someday, perhaps, would have found himself driving a late-model stock car. But since he was in the Midwest, he wound up around sprint cars. Dozens of dirt and paved tracks dot the countryside in Indiana and Ohio, and hardly a night goes by between Easter and Labor Day that sprint and midget cars aren't running somewhere.

Richmond started working on cars driven by Dave Shoemaker and going to the track on weekends. Shoemaker had half ownership in the team and a friend of Al Richmond's owned the other half.

"Dave doesn't like this story, but it's true," Richmond said in a 1985 interview. "We were at a race one night and during intermission our friend told Dave to let me try to drive the car."

It was in 1976, when Richmond was 21 years old. The track was Lakeville Speedway in Lakeville, Ohio. Cars were allowed on the track between portions of the weekly show, and Tim got talked into giving Shoemaker's car a whirl.

"Somebody put a stopwatch on me," Richmond said. "I was running laps faster than Dave had been. It was the first time I had ever driven a race car."

Richmond was hooked.

He and his father began looking for a sprint car they could buy and get ready for Richmond to go racing in. The very idea of Tim climbing into a race car mortified Evelyn, and that probably made Al more determined to go through with the plan. Racing would be a way for the father to bond with a son who always had been so much closer to his mother.

Al and Tim found a car for sale in Mercer, Pennsylvania, and got on the plane and flew over to take a look. The car was painted red, white and blue and had the No. 98 on it. When growing up, Richmond had built numerous model cars and he painted all of them red, white and blue and put "98" on them.

"I had to have it," Tim said.

The Richmonds flew back to Ohio, then Tim drove back to Pennsylvania to tow home his new toy on a trailer hooked to a pickup. He got it ready to race and towed it back to the track in Mercer. Richmond borrowed a fire suit from one of the drag racer buddies he'd met through his friendship with Miller.

Since Richmond was new to the track, he was automatically placed in the slowest heat. It turned out not to be a particularly glorious career debut.

Richmond passed a car on the first lap he ran, then passed another on the second. On his third lap, however, Richmond lost control coming out of Turn 2. As he started to spin, he remembered something he'd heard people tell Shoemaker—stand on the gas, spin the car 360-degrees and keep going. So Richmond stood on it and spun 360 degrees—and kept right on spinning.

With his car still whirling, Richmond looked out of the open cockpit and saw another car coming out of Turn 2. "It was so far back, I didn't think there would be any problem missing me," Richmond said. "I turned my head and tried to get my car headed in the right direction." The on-coming car hit Richmond's car in the left front. The blow turned Richmond the way he needed to be going, so he floored the throttle again and took off.

But during the spin, a suspension part had been damaged. "I hadn't gone very far when the axle that keeps the car from shifting back and forth and left and right broke," Richmond said. "All of a sudden the axle shifted to the right of the car, and it turned right and started spinning again. So I hit the throttle and did another 360 and came out straight. I hit the throttle again and the car veered to the right, not real hard, but now it's headed toward the bank that was right by the third turn. By this time they've already thrown the caution. I've spun out twice and I'm over the bank. The car shifts left and here I come back over the bank over Turn 3. The axle goes a little bit more to the left and I start to spin again.

"I stand on it again and whoooom! The car comes all the way around and is facing straight again. I was good at that, I guess. I hit the throttle and the axle goes back to the right and I spin again. Finally after four spins and one trip over the bank I think, 'There might be something wrong with this car.'"

Al Richmond saw the whirling dervish his son had become and was just hoping that eventually Tim would make it to pit road. The Richmonds had bought spare parts when they bought the car, and repairs on the axle could have been made in relatively short order. But Al had seen enough for one night.

Richmond later towed his car to the famed Eldora Speedway near Rossburg, Ohio, a high-banked half-mile dirt oval that to this day is one of the most revered race courses in the Midwest. He crashed again, and Al decided that the Richmond family sprint car team needed to fire its driver.

Before the 1977 racing season, Al bought his son a super-modified and that turned out to be a much better fit. Richmond raced that year at a track in Sandusky, Ohio, and wound up winning rookie of the year and the track championship in his class. He moved up to the U.S. Auto Club's sprint car series in 1978, running 12 races with a best finish of fourth at Salem, Indiana. He finished 30th in points and was named rookie of the year. He also attended a road-course driving school run by Jim Russell at Willow Springs Raceway in California and proved to be so adept that by the end of his instruction he'd set a course record for students.

Perhaps most significantly, Richmond also went to Phoenix International Raceway and ran a race in the Mini Indy-car series. Driving a Lola 620, he won the support event to an Indy-car race to put his name in front of some of the most important car owners in America's top open-wheel series.

So by 1979, just three years after he had first climbed into a race car, Richmond's career was already pointing toward the premiere racing event in the United States—the Indianapolis 500. While other drivers spent years banging around in sprint cars trying to get an opportunity to step up to the sport's highest level, Richmond had several factors working in his favor that accelerated his process.

First, of course, there was every indication he had the basic driving talent. Second, while his father had enough money to buy his son an Indy-car ride, Richmond had an intuitive understanding that sponsorship dollars were the sport's mother's milk. And he found that his good looks and personal charisma helped attract people with money who were willing to help him pursue his dream. Among those were a couple from his hometown of Ashland, Bob and Vera Schultz, who read about the young man's rise through racing's ranks and decided they wanted to get involved in helping him continue his climb.

With backing from the Schultzes and his father, along with some advice from racing mogul Roger Penske, who'd been among those to see him drive the Mini-Indy cars, Richmond worked out

a deal to buy an Indy car and prepared to make his debut at
Michigan International Speedway in July. He drove car No. 69 with
an Eagle chassis and an Offenhauser engine to a qualifying lap of
175.768 mph, the 21st fastest time posted. Bobby Unser won the
pole at 203.879 mph, so Richmond's car clearly was outclassed in
terms of power. He lasted just four laps before blowing his engine,
finishing 23rd—last among the cars that took the green flag.

Even though it was a short day and a tough weekend,
Richmond's presence and the flashes of ability he showed given
the level of equipment he'd managed to put underneath him stoked
interest in his career. A team owned by Pat Santello and sponsored
by S&M Electric had been using Larry Rice as its driver but was
looking for someone new. The next race on the Indy Car schedule
was at Watkins Glen, an historic road course in upstate New York
that would over the next decade have a remarkable way of factor-
ing into Richmond's life and career. Santello and Mark Stainbook,
the team's chief mechanic, decided to give Richmond a test that,
ironically, was scheduled for the Willow Springs road course in
California—where Richmond had attended the Jim Russell driving school and done so well.

Richmond "passed" the test and went to Watkins Glen for the
Kent Oil 150 on August 5. He qualified 15th fastest at 119.523 mph,
again well off Al Unser's pole speed of 135.657 mph. Al Unser and
Bobby Unser swapped the lead all day, but Richmond made his
way up to eighth and finished 58 of the 62 laps for what would be
the best career finish in an Indy Car event.

Richmond ran three more races later that year and was already
trying to put together his own team for the 1980 season.

He ran into a man named Robert Tezak, whom he'd met the
previous year when Richmond was driving the Mini-Indy car. "We
just sort of hit it off real well and became friends," Tezak said. "I
had followed him and knew he was racing."

Richmond asked Tezak if he knew any company that might be interested in sponsoring an Indy Car team.

"I might," Tezak said.

CHAPTER 3

There was something odd, Richmond admitted later, about the first time he talked to Bob Tezak about making a deal to go to the Indianapolis 500.

"I said to myself, 'Don't be rude, Richmond, but this guy is a coroner,'" he said. "'That doesn't go very well with a race car.'"

Tezak was the coroner in Will County, one of six counties that make up the Chicago metropolitan area. The county seat of Joliet, about 40 miles south of Chicago, would in the late 1990s become home to the Chicagoland Speedway, where NASCAR holds races each season.

In 1971, a few years after he'd graduated from junior college in Joliet, Tezak was visiting relatives in Kentucky and started playing a card game he found entertaining. He bought the rights to the game, called UNO, from its inventor and began marketing it from the home he shared with his wife, Sandra, and Mark, her son from a previous marriage. Tezak and two other family members soon founded International Games to manufacture and sell the game. They sold 15,000 sets in 1974, but by 1980 nearly 10 million sets of

UNO were sold. The success helped Tezak gain entry into Will County Republican Party politics and, in 1976 at the age of 28, he was elected coroner and started to become a major player in the GOP's operations.

By the end of 1979, Al Richmond and the Schultzes were looking to put together a team for Tim for 1980. When Tezak joined the effort, things began to come together.

"Tim had a marvelous personality," Tezak said. "He had everything it took to be a superstar, and by that I am talking about a lot more than driving. He had raw talent coming out of his ears, but he had a lot more than that. He had the personality; he knew how to treat people and how to talk to people. He was just a regular person. Everybody loved him for that. He got along with a fan who walked in off the street who had never been to a race before all the way up to Roger Penske."

Penske sold the team a car, a Penske PC-7 chassis, basically a 1979 iteration of the superteam's Indy Car model. Richmond picked up additional sponsorship from an Indianapolis radio station and, in the No. 21 UNO Q95 Starcruiser, the rookie driver immediately began to make his mark.

"It was just incredible," Tezak said. "It was like somebody's dream. Things just don't happen that way—we were just fast from the word go."

Things were in a state of flux at Indianapolis in 1980. Championship Auto Racing Teams and the U.S. Auto Club had forged a tenuous union to oversee open-wheel racing, calling it the Championship Racing League. The CRL would last just five races, but the 1980 Indy 500 was held under its aegis. Rules were also changing. In 1978, Tom Sneva had become the first driver to average more than 200 mph for a four-lap qualifying effort at Indianapolis, running 202.156 mph to win the pole. New rules for 1979 slowed speeds significantly, with pole winner Rick Mears averaging 193.736 mph.

In the week before 1980 qualifying opened, Richmond topped the 193 mph mark on a practice lap—the fastest speed in pre-qualifying runs. The question, Indianapolis Motor Speedway historian Donald Davidson said, is whether the car could have made it through inspection in that condition.

"The team could have posted that lap for psychological reasons," Davidson said. "At any rate, Tim was certainly going around telling everybody how fast they were. He was just amazing with the press. He was on top of the world. All of the television stations wanted to talk to him at the end of the day and somebody asked him if they were legal. Tim said yes. John Barnes was the team's chief mechanic. He'd been around the sport but he was pretty new as a chief mechanic. I said to Barnes, 'That's a great lap, and Tim said it was legal.' Barnes said, 'Tim talks too much.' I don't know what that meant."

Even though Richmond was a rookie, he was no stranger to Davidson and others around Indianapolis—the city and the track. "I think it was 1978 or 1979, but he went to the victory banquet with Linda Vaughn and two other of the Hurst girls," Davidson said. Vaughn was—and still today is—known as "Miss Hurst Shifter" after winning a national contest to earn the right to represent Hurst's gear-shifting products in advertisements and at racing events. Richmond and Vaughn would remain friends for the balance of Richmond's career. Tezak had a home in Claremont, Indiana, not far from the track in Speedway, and Richmond got an apartment close to the track for the activities that lasted for the entire month of May leading up to the 500.

"Tim was around a lot, riding a bicycle through the garage or going out on his motorcycle," Davidson said. "Back then they had charity softball games with drivers and the mechanics and he played in those. He was in the middle of all of that. He was always part of the social functions. He had a real following before he ever went to the speedway because he was around town a whole lot."

Richmond enjoyed the off-track activities, but Tezak said any stories that Richmond was out all hours partying were exaggerated.

"What do you consider a party?" Tezak said. "Going out to dinner and having a couple of beers? That's all part of the sport. You can't lock yourself in your room and not see anybody until you go to the track the next day. Part of being successful is being out, talking to people and associating with them. Tim absolutely wanted to be liked and recognized, and he worked at it. He wanted to be recognized by not only Roger Penske and Bill France, but he wanted the fan who just walked through the gate for the first time to like him, too."

Richmond's fast car never got a chance to challenge for the pole for the 1980 Indianapolis 500, which Johnny Rutherford won with a four-lap average of 192.256 mph. Richmond hit the wall on the morning of the first qualifying day, damaging the car enough that the team had to get another Penske car ready for the second weekend of qualifying. The backup wasn't as fast as the original, but it was still plenty fast. Richmond posted a four-lap average of 188.334 mph, the fifth best overall speed. Because he didn't qualify until the second weekend, however, Richmond was relegated to the 19th starting spot.

There were a couple of reasons the press spent as much time as they did that month talking about and to Richmond.

First, he was the new kid in town. He was young, he was good-looking and he had an intuitive understanding that reporters would flock to somebody who was both relevant, because his fast car was worthy of note, and interesting. While other drivers, especially irascible veterans like A.J. Foyt, didn't necessarily enjoy the time they spent talking to reporters, Richmond ate up the attention.

"Things were very different in those days than what they are now for drivers at the 500 or in NASCAR," Davidson said. "In those days, the drivers could come and go around the track and around the city. People would cheer them, but they wouldn't get mobbed like they do now."

Richmond was a fresh story, offering reporters new ground to be plowed. The young man from right next door in Ohio also gave people covering the 500 something other than Johnny Rutherford to write about. "Rutherford was so clearly the favorite that year, I don't remember there being a lot of prerace talk about who could win the 500," Davidson said. "By February or March, even, it seemed that running the race was just a formality."

Rutherford, who'd won the 500 in 1974 and 1976, had won the pole by going more than 1 mph over his four laps than second best qualifier Mario Andretti. Being faster in qualifying doesn't necessarily mean superiority in the race, but all month long, Rutherford's car had been the most consistently fast machine on the famed 2.5-mile oval. By Monday, May 26—race day—the Texan was clearly favored to win his third 500.

"Rutherford was routinely running 190 mph laps in the race," Davidson said. "Sneva was running second and his best lap might have been 184 mph." Sneva had started last, 33rd, after wrecking the car he'd qualified during practice and going to a backup. But his team used strategy well enough to get him up through the field. Caution flags—there were 13 of them for 64 laps by day's end—fell fortuitously as well, allowing Sneva to at least stay on the same lap with Rutherford.

"If the race had stayed green all the way," Davidson said, "Rutherford would have lapped the field several times."

Richmond, meanwhile, worked his way up, eventually getting into the top five. As he dove off the track to make a pit stop on Lap 73, Richmond actually crossed the scoring line ahead of Rutherford and was credited for leading that lap—the only lap he would ever lead in the Indianapolis 500. Rutherford passed Bobby Unser on Lap 104 and began to assert his dominance. He led all but 15 of the final 96 laps and won by 29.9 seconds over Sneva.

Once again, however, Richmond found a way to put himself alongside Rutherford—quite literally—in the headline moment of the race.

Richmond had been trying to make his last load of fuel last until the checkered flag, but he came up short. Just as his car crossed the start-finish line after completing 197 laps, the UNO Q95 Starcruiser's engine sputtered to a stop. Richmond coasted almost all the way around the track, but came to a stop on the apron leading to pit road coming off the fourth turn.

Rutherford and the rest of the field, meanwhile, were completing the race, with Sneva, Gary Bettenhausen and Gordon Johncock also completing all 200 laps. Rick Mears, Pancho Carter, Danny Ongais and Tom Bigelow also were scored ahead of Richmond's stalled car, giving Richmond a ninth-place finish.

"As the car was rolling to a stop, I imagine I'm hearing a dull roar," Richmond said in a 1985 interview. "I couldn't look around but I thought the crowd might be clapping for me. So I sort of stuck my hand up out of the car and the noise got tremendously louder. I thought, 'This is pretty neat.' So I stuck my whole arm out of the car and the crowd went nuts. 'Yahoo!' I unhooked my belts and the car was still rolling a bit, and I jumped out just before it came to a complete stop. The crowd loved it and made more noise. Now I'm standing there waving to the people."

What Richmond didn't realize was that the crowd was cheering for Rutherford, who was completing his victory lap after taking the checkered flag and rolling up behind him on the track.

"He had stopped but I didn't see him," Richmond said. "I was still playing up to the crowd. I looked and there was Rutherford, waving for me to jump on his car."

Rutherford's team had been in a garage adjacent to Richmond's team during May's activities, and sufficient goodwill had come of that situation that Rutherford was willing to give the rookie driver a lift back to the garage. Richmond climbed onto the side pod of

Rutherford's yellow No. 4 Chaparral race car, looping his arm through the roll cage to hold on as they rode down pit road toward the winners' circle at Indianapolis Motor Speedway—perhaps the most sacred ground in all of American auto racing.

"That had to be one of the great moments, ever," Davidson said. "It's a forever highlight. Tim was hanging on with one hand and, with his right hand, pointing his finger into the cockpit toward Rutherford. They stopped, just before making the turn into victory circle, and Tim got off. He kind of just disappeared into the crowd as they pushed Rutherford's car in. I guess he just walked back down toward his pit."

The rookie of the year award for the Indianapolis 500 does not automatically go to the first-year driver who posts the best finish in the race. A panel selects the winner, but Richmond was the best rookie finisher and was a clear choice.

"He thoroughly deserved the award," Davidson said with a chuckle. "One of the criteria they use is cooperation with the press, and in that, he may have been the best there has ever been."

Richmond's future in open-wheel racing seemed boundless. "He looked like he was going to be what a guy like Rick Mears ended up being," Davidson said. "He had all of the talent and all of the personality. You figured he'd end up driving for the Penske team because they'd bought their cars from Penske."

But Richmond's fortunes soon took an abrupt turn for the worse. He wrecked in qualifying for the next race at Milwaukee on June 8. He wrecked again at Mid-Ohio in July and didn't complete a lap. Then, on July 20, in the Norton 200 at Michigan International Speedway, Richmond crashed after completing just four laps. It was a savage wreck, with his car basically torn apart from the impact with the wall.

Evelyn Richmond had seen enough.

"Mother was in Florida at the condo," Sandy Welsh said. "She didn't want him racing and she couldn't stand to watch it. But she was watching it on TV. I was in Ashland. This car comes apart and she calls on the phone. She was absolutely hysterical, screaming and carrying on."

The next time Evelyn saw Al Richmond, she put her foot down.

"She told Al, 'You get him out of that car, or I will divorce you and I will take every penny you have,'" Welsh said. "And she said, 'If something happens to Tim, I'll kill you.'

"And she was not joking."

CHAPTER 4

One spectator watching Richmond run the Indianapolis 500 was a dentist from Pennsylvania named Joe Mattioli.

Mattioli owned Pocono Raceway, a 2.5-mile triangular-shaped track in the Pocono Mountains that in those days hosted both Indy Car and NASCAR Winston Cup series events each year. Mattioli thought Richmond might bring some fans into his track's NASCAR event, one of only eight Cup races held that season at tracks located outside stock-car racing's bastion of support in the Southeast.

Mario Andretti, A.J. Foyt and Dan Gurney were among the open-wheel stars who had come over to NASCAR and won races, with Andretti and Foyt both winning the circuit's biggest race, the Daytona 500, Andretti in 1967 and Foyt in 1972. But there was still a gap to be bridged between the two disciplines.

"Stock car racing was still very much a Southern sport then, and some of the people in NASCAR didn't take kindly to Northerners unless they had the right kind of personality," Davidson said. "When I first heard that Tim was going down there to race, though, I wasn't worried about him. I knew he had enough 'B.S.' that people would accept him anywhere."

Pocono was an interesting choice for Richmond to make his first NASCAR start. No other stock car track is anything like it. The frontstretch, a 3,740-foot straightaway, leads to Turn 1 that is banked at 14 degrees and acts like a turn at one of the circuit's larger, high-speed ovals. From there, another 3,055-foot straightaway connects to Turn 2, called the "Tunnel Turn" because it sits on top of a tunnel that allows access to the track's vast infield. The turn has only eight degrees of banking and is a notoriously treacherous corner that's more like one found on a short track. The third straightaway is only 1,780 feet—still nearly three times longer than the straightaways at Bristol—and leads to a sharp, Turn 3 that, with four degrees of banking, is like turns found on a road course. Since cars can't be built or set up to race optimally on a superspeedway, a short track and a road course at the same time, Pocono offers a unique challenge. A team can give its driver a compromise and depend on him to do the rest, and often it takes a few visits for even the most talented drivers to get a good handle on it.

With Mattioli's help, Richmond and Bob Tezak put together a deal with D.K. Ulrich, one of the sport's independent car owners. Ulrich had been running in NASCAR's top series since 1971 and would, over 25 seasons, enter cars in 545 races. In 1980 alone, 14 different drivers drove Ulrich-owned cars in Cup races. Richmond would join drivers like Lennie Pond, J.D. McDuffie, Ricky Rudd and Sterling Marlin on that list. He showed up at Pocono and qualified 23rd fastest, meaning he'd line up for the start of the Coca-Cola 500 directly behind Janet Guthrie, a female driver who'd also come to national attention by entering the Indianapolis 500 and who would be making her 33rd and, as it turned out, final Cup start in the July 27 race.

Driving the No. 40 Chevrolet, with sponsorship from Tezak's UNO card game as well as from the Caesars Pocono Resorts,

Richmond completed 195 of the scheduled 200 laps and acquitted himself nicely, finishing 12th in a race won by Neil Bonnett. Richmond's winnings were $3,965. Dale Earnhardt, in his second year of NASCAR Winston Cup competition, finished fourth that day and left Pocono with a 144-point lead in the championship standings.

Harry Dinwiddie drove Ulrich's No. 40 in the next Cup race at Talladega, then Ulrich took over in it for the next four events. Richmond returned at Dover, Delaware, on September 14 and qualified 17th in a 40-car field. He completed just 258 of the 500 laps in the CRC Chemicals 500 at the one-mile track, going out with a bad cylinder head in a race Darrell Waltrip won.

Richmond's third start came at Martinsville Speedway, a .525-mile short track in southern Virginia that's shaped like a paper clip. It's basically two 800-foot dragstrips connected at each end by sharp turns with 12 degrees of banking. A racing lap there consists of going as fast as possible from one end to the next, then slowing as rapidly as possible to negotiate the next turn. In the Old Dominion 500 on September 28, Richmond started 20th in a 31-car field. He finished 12th again, matching his Pocono finish, completing 469 laps to finish 31 laps behind Earnhardt.

The next race, on October 5, was at Charlotte Motor Speedway. Now called Lowe's Motor Speedway, the 1.5-mile Charlotte track is the sport's prototypical intermediate oval. Buddy Baker won the pole for the National 500 at better than 165 mph, with Richmond starting back in 21st. He finished 12th again, and Earnhardt won again, as he tried to protect his lead in the championship standings.

Richmond's final race of 1980 came at Atlanta Motor Speedway, then a 1.522-mile oval, in the Atlanta Journal 500 on November 2. Ulrich entered two cars in that race, with Richmond driving the No. 6 Chevrolet. He started 32nd and finished 29th, going out early with clutch problems.

The significance of that race in Richmond's life stems from the story of the other Ulrich car entered that day. The No. 40 was driven by Stan Barrett, a professional driver and Hollywood stunt man who a year earlier set the unofficial land speed record of 739.666 mph in a rocket-powered, aluminum-wheeled car. Barrett was racing Ulrich's cars with the backing of movie director Hal Needham and actor Burt Reynolds, Needham's close friend and the star of several of the director's films. Barrett finished 10th that day in the second of his three starts for Ulrich in 1980, and would run 10 races the following year in cars owned by Needham, splitting time in the '81 season with Harry Gant, a veteran of NASCAR's second-tier series. U.S. Tobacco would come aboard as that team's sponsor, using NASCAR to promote its "Skoal Bandit" brand.

Gant would go on to become one of the sport's most popular drivers, winning for the first time at Martinsville in 1982 at the age of 42. To this day, nobody in NASCAR's top series has ever been older when he won his first race. The success and acceptance Needham, Reynolds and Gant enjoyed led directly to the idea for a stock-car racing movie called *Stroker Ace*, starring Reynolds with Loni Anderson, Jim Nabors and Ned Beatty along with dozens of people connected to NASCAR, including drivers Dale Earnhardt, Terry Labonte, Ricky Rudd and Tim Richmond.

Though a great deal of what Richmond filmed for the movie wound up on the editing room floor, he enjoyed the process. The concept of playing a role appealed to him, as did the attention he undoubtedly saw lavished on stars like Reynolds and the blonde and buxom Anderson during the filming.

But at the end of the 1980, Richmond was still a racer. Evelyn wasn't completely mollified to have her son out of Indy cars, but stock cars certainly looked more substantial and at least gave her the illusion that Tim had more to protect him than what she'd seen when his car came apart with him in it at Michigan.

Stock car racing had a definite appeal for Richmond, too. He'd certainly shown the same raw talent that had first got him noticed in open-wheel circles. But he was an outsider in a sport that in those days, frankly, didn't exactly rush to welcome them.

The 1981 NASCAR Winston Cup schedule included 31 races, and 22 of them were to be run in the Carolinas, Virginia, Tennessee, Georgia, Florida and Alabama. NASCAR had a solid fan following in those Southeastern states, and pockets of support in other parts of the country—such as Michigan, where two races were held at the same track where Indy cars ran near the town of Brooklyn. But stock car racing was still in its infancy as a television sport. Just two years earlier, in fact, CBS had telecast the Daytona 500 live from start to finish for the first time ever. The sport was still primarily a regional one, and its fans and many of its drivers were Southerners by birth—and proud of it.

There were two typical styles of dress in the NASCAR garage in those days. Mechanics who worked on the cars wore the kind of clothes they would have worn to work at the local filling station— mostly plain white T-shirts with dungarees. The drivers, who had a little more money and, most often a lot more ego, came to the track in blue jeans with a Western-style shirt and, in many cases, cowboy boots with a matching hat. It was the "Urban Cowboy" look, patterned after the popular 1980 film starring John Travolta.

Richmond, however, rode Hogs—Harley-Davidson motorcycles—not horses. He had his own style.

"One time I told my wife, 'Find out who does his hair,'" fellow driver Buddy Baker once said. "'It looks better than yours does.'"

Tom Higgins, who spent more than 30 years covering the sport before retiring as the NASCAR beat writer for *The Charlotte Observer* in 1997, remembers the first time he saw Richmond.

"The Charlotte speedway was having a press conference," Higgins recalled. "I pulled up and parked and the first person I saw was D.K. Ulrich. I was sort of surprised, because D.K. didn't make it to many press conferences. He had this guy with him who looked like somebody who'd stepped out of *GQ Magazine*. He had on a red blazer, with white slacks and white shoes. His hair was perfect and he had a deep tan. He was a real dandy. I said, 'Who in God's name is this?' He looked like a movie star. We got in and they did their little announcements and everything, and then they had D.K. introduce his new driver. And it was Tim Richmond."

Barry Dodson, who would later become Richmond's crew chief and one of his best friends, had a similar first impression.

"The first time I saw Tim was over at Charlotte," Dodson said. "He was driving the car for D.K. and he had on this flashy driving suit. Looking at him, he reminded you more of Evel Knievel than a race car driver. Everybody thought, 'Who is this guy?'"

Most drivers in NASCAR at the time were either sons of the South or people who'd worked their way into familiarity in stock car circles by racing at the few tracks outside the region when NASCAR visited. There were drivers who came to NASCAR from the Midwest, but most of them had raced in the U.S. Auto Club's stock car series and therefore had at least those credentials to present upon entry to the good ol' boys' club.

"When Tim came in he really didn't know anybody, and nobody knew him," said Chip Williams, who started as NASCAR's media relations director in 1981 and worked with Richmond that year in the sport's rookie driver program. "He was seen as an outsider . . . and people just didn't make friends as quickly back then. It's different now; you can come into NASCAR from anywhere. But back then, if you were an outsider, you had to kind of earn your way into the family.

"Tim tried to come in kind of the same way Darrell Waltrip did. It was like neither of them felt like they needed to earn their way in. They wanted to come right in and be one of the kingpins and let their talent do all of the talking. That's not how it was at that time. Nobody could do that, no matter how good you were. You had to work your way up so people felt like you deserved your shot at NASCAR."

Williams said rookies were told that if they encountered any problems or had any questions about how things were done in the sport, they could go to NASCAR or to one of the sport's veteran drivers for advice.

"They could go up to Richard Petty or Bobby Allison and those guys would stop and help," Williams said. "And if a rookie did that, those veterans were then more apt to cut them a break on the race track. But Richmond didn't go ask for that kind of help, and some people saw that as him sort of trying to bully his way in instead of earning his way."

There simply was no natural fit for Richmond in the sport.

"There was no slot for a silk suit-wearing guy with Italian loafers who comes to Darlington or Bristol and jumps in a stock car and kicks everybody's rear end," said Kyle Petty, who also wore his hair a lot longer than the average NASCAR driver in those days, but who had two generations of family history to make that feat easier to pull off. "That was not normal. People were asking who he was and where did he come from. Tim wanted to win races and beat Dale Earnhardt and those cats, but he also liked being who he was."

Kyle Petty is the son of the sport's all-time winningest driver, Richard Petty, and the grandson of Lee Petty, one of NASCAR's most dominant drivers in the sport's early days. Kyle had run five races in 1979 and 10 more in 1980 in the Cup series, and began the 1981 season planning to run a full season. Richmond had made a similar choice. He started the year in a No. 99 Chevrolet owned by Ulrich, but engine problems left him 29th on the road course at Riverside, California, in the last race in which NASCAR teams were allowed to run cars with a 115-inch wheelbase. Beginning with the Daytona 500, the rules would require teams to use cars five inches shorter because American automobile manufacturers were "downsizing" their production vehicles upon which the "stock" cars were supposedly based.

The change complicated preparations for the 1981 season for even the most highly funded teams, and Ulrich's team certainly wasn't among those. So there was little surprise when Richmond's No. 99 Buick Regal finished 30th after he started 40th in the Daytona 500. Richmond fell out with transmission trouble after 144 laps. He crashed out at Atlanta in the season's fifth race, too, but finally got his first career top-10 finish with a 10th at Bristol.

Later he came home sixth at Talladega and 12th at Nashville before skipping the Cup races at Dover and Charlotte to return for another try at the Indianapolis 500. Coming off his rookie of the year performance from 1980, hopes were high, but he qualified at 185.309 mph, well off Bobby Unser's pole speed of 200.546 mph, and on the final day of qualifications saw the No. 21 UNO-sponsored car get bumped from the field.

"When it was over, he had missed the show," Davidson said. "But his people wanted him in the race, so they went to A.J. Foyt to see if they could put him in the car that George Snider had qualified. They went to Snider and offered him a sum of money to give up the car and he did." Richmond started at the rear of the field as a substitute driver. He was running at the end of the day, but finished 14th in Unser's victory and was never much of a factor.

Richmond's career as an open-wheel driver ended with that race. He'd bought a house on Lake Norman near Mooresville, N.C., a town just north of Charlotte where the vast majority of NASCAR teams had their headquarters. It was time for Richmond to move to the South and start winning races—and winning over those people who still didn't quite yet know what to make of him.

CHAPTER 5

The 2004 NASCAR Nextel Cup season consisted of 36 points races plus a pair of non-points events, stretching from early February until mid-November—the longest season in professional sports.

In 1981, the 31-race season actually ran even longer. The first and last races of the season were at Riverside, California, with the opener on January 11 and the finale on November 22. There were more open dates on that schedule than there are today, and more races were bunched closer together geographically in the Southeast. On the other hand, teams weren't flying around in private jets and carrying their cars to the track in $1 million transporters that serve as a shop on wheels in those days, either.

The pace was still grueling and, except for a few of the teams with the absolute top level of funding, the cars the drivers raced in on Sunday were all-purpose machines used on virtually every style of track.

There certainly were more good drivers in the sport than there were good teams. In 2001, a record 19 different drivers won Cup races. From 1994 through 2003, at least 14 different drivers won at least one race in each of those seasons. But from the beginning of the sport's so-called "modern era" in 1972—when Winston became the top circuit's primary sponsor, tracks shorter than a half-mile were dropped, and the schedule was pared from as many as 55 races in a year to around 30—it took until 1988 before as many as 14 drivers won races in the same year. From 1972 to 1987, the average number of different winners per season was nine. Over that span, an average of nearly 75 percent of all races were won each year by just three or four top teams.

D.K. Ulrich's team was never going to be one of those teams. In 545 starts over his career as a car owner, Ulrich himself drove to the only top-five finish he'd ever score when he finished fourth at Dover in 1981 while Richmond was off running the Indianapolis 500.

Richmond returned to NASCAR at College Station, Texas, on June 7, and finished seventh in a race won by Benny Parsons. But the next Sunday at Riverside Richmond crashed out after completing just 12 laps and finished 33rd. Richmond had qualified no higher than 13th in his 13 starts for Ulrich that year, but he'd finished in the top 10 three times. He'd done well enough for some people around the sport to get over their initial skepticism.

"I had been around the sport a long time, and we had seen dozens of people come through, guys who were all going to be the next great thing," Tom Higgins said. "You'd see one of those guys and say, 'Yeah, he'll be down here until the money runs out and then he'll be gone.' But Richmond was taking mediocre cars and running pretty well in them. You just got the sense he was going to be a good driver, especially if he got with a team that could give him some equipment that would last."

Still, Richmond had not finished on the lead lap in 18 races over two seasons in Ulrich's cars. He wanted more, and when a racer is convinced that the car he's driving is holding him back—

whether that perception is true or not—he starts looking for another place to race.

Immediately after Riverside, Richmond jumped to the No. 12 cars owned by Kennie Childers. Donnie Allison and Harry Gant had each driven for Childers in three races earlier that year, and David Pearson had put the team's Oldsmobile on the pole at Dover and led 41 laps before blowing an engine. If nothing else, Richmond could make himself believe that Pearson's pole showed there was speed in Childers's car. Richmond ran the No. 12 Olds at Michigan, finishing two laps down in 14th, and was 15th at Daytona in the team's Buick. At Nashville on July 11, Richmond drove a No. 75 Chevrolet owned by Bob Rahilly and Butch Mock for their RahMoc team and qualified sixth, his best starting spot so far. He finished 12th. Then, in his first trip back to Pocono since his stock-car debut the previous year, Richmond finished ninth back in Childers's Oldsmobile.

Very few people, however, were paying much attention to what was going on with Richmond that summer. One week after Richmond left Ulrich's team, the NASCAR Winston Cup world was rocked when Rod Osterlund sold the team with which Dale Earnhardt had won the 1980 championship. The sale of the reigning champion's team in the middle of a season was a big deal anyway, but this story was made even bigger by the name of the man who'd bought it.

J.D. (Jim) Stacy had cut a swath through the sport several years earlier, bringing a fortune he'd earned in coal mining in Kentucky when he bought out Nord Krauskopf's team in 1977. Krauskopf's team had won more than 40 races and the 1970 championship with Bobby Isaac before, at the end of 1976, longtime sponsor K&K Insurance pulled out. Harry Hyde was crew chief for Isaac during the championship season and was still there when Neil Bonnett took over in 1977 with the team grabbing up sponsor dollars wherever it could. After the World 600 in May, Krauskopf gave up and

Stacy purchased the team. Bonnett won the pole at Daytona in July in the team's first race, then got his first career victory at Richmond in September in the No. 5 Dodge in his fifth start with Stacy as car owner. Bonnett won again in the final race of 1977 at Ontario, California, a victory in a Dodge that would be the last for a Chrysler product until after Dodge made its return to the sport in 2001.

The following year, however, Bonnett went winless, and the team began to come apart. Stacy's money wasn't always getting to the people it was owed to. A second team Stacy planned to launch made only two starts, and its driver, Ferrel Harris, and Hyde both went to court to get money they believed they were entitled to.

Stacy dropped out of sight. There was a story that he had seen some suspicious wires dangling from beneath his car and, when he checked them, found the car had been rigged to explode. What people in racing new for sure, though, was that neither Stacy nor the money he'd promised people was around any more.

But in 1981 he was back again. On June 26, he paid $1.7 million for Osterlund's team and its equipment. Earnhardt, the 1979 rookie of the year who then won the championship in his second season, was as stunned as the rest of the racing world. He lasted four races with Stacy as his car owner. After the No. 2 Pontiac Earnhardt drove in the Talladega 500 on August 2 lost a transmission and Earnhardt finished 29th, he took the Wrangler Jeans sponsorship and moved into the No. 3 Pontiacs that independent owner/driver Richard Childress had been driving. It would not be until 1984 that Earnhardt and Childress would reunite permanently, but the seeds for one of the greatest partnerships in NASCAR history were planted.

When Earnhardt left, Joe Ruttman took over in Stacy's car and finished the season. Richmond, meanwhile, drove eight races for Childers before moving again, this time to a team owned by Bob Rogers. Richmond started fifth at Charlotte and sixth in the finale at Riverside but blew three engines and crashed once in his seven starts with Rogers. He finished his rookie season with six top-10 finishes in 29 starts, earning $96,448 and finishing 16th in the points standings. Ron Bouchard finished 21st in the points, mainly because he made only 22 starts, but he still was named rookie of the year over Richmond after winning on August 2 at Talladega in a Buick owned by Jack Beebe. Bouchard also won a pole at Michigan and had five top-five finishes and 12 top 10s.

On paper, Richmond was left with little to show from that rookie campaign. But he did run nearly 9,100 miles in a stock car, and every one of those was valuable to a driver who was still only 26 years old when the season ended.

What he didn't have at the start of the 1982 season, however, was a ride. Earnhardt had gone to the Bud Moore-owned Fords. Ricky Rudd had stepped in to drive for Richard Childress. And, in one way or another, most everybody else was racing for J.D. Stacy. Ruttman was still driving the No. 2 car in which he'd replaced Earnhardt the year before. Now he had a teammate—Jim Sauter in the No. 5. But that wasn't enough for Stacy. He also was the primary sponsor for five other cars, driven by Bouchard, Terry Labonte, Dave Marcis, Benny Parsons and Jody Ridley.

Seeing Stacy's name still made Harry Hyde's blood boil. Hyde had been part of something great with Nord Krauskopf's team. In 1969, he and Bobby Isaac had won 19 poles and 17 of the season's 50 races. The next year, they'd won 11 races, 13 poles and a championship. When Stacy came along, all of that fell apart. Hyde, at one point, found himself locked out of his own shop. He had gone all but broke as he fought in court to get back money he believed Stacy owed him and, like Richmond, Hyde found himself without a racing home when the 1981 season ended.

That's how Richmond and Hyde wound up together for the first time, in 1982, trying to get their car into the Daytona 500. Richmond had signed on to drive and Hyde was the crew chief for a team called Fast Company Ltd., and was owned by William J. (Billie) Harvey, a 32-year-old from Georgia who also was driving another car entered in the Daytona 500.

The field for NASCAR's biggest race is set primarily based on the results of 125-mile qualifying races held the Thursday before the 500. Richmond didn't finish well enough to earn a spot in the main event, and the speed he had posted didn't make the cut, either. Richmond won a "consolation" race held for those who hadn't made the 500 field, but there was very little consolation in that "win."

The 500 was held on February 14, but four days after it, Bobby Allison's victory was wiped off the front pages of sports sections across the Southeast with news of indictments of 70 people in a $300 million drug-smuggling operation. Among those indicted were Harvey, Gary Balough, who'd finished 11th in the Daytona 500, and Tom Pistone, who'd finished fourth in the consolation race Richmond had won. The indictments stemmed from an investigation lasting more than two years in which police had tracked drugs smuggled into Florida from the Bahamas and, in at least one case, stashed in a race car and towed on a trailer across a state line. Some of the indictments were against mechanics who, in addition to tuning race cars, worked on powerboats that brought the marijuana and cocaine ashore. Police said the operation had been in existence for at least five years.

Richmond made it onto the track with Fast Company just one time, at Rockingham in late March, but Richmond's engine blew after 112 laps, and he finished 31st in a 34-car field. The demise of the race team was not the best news in the world for Richmond, of course. But he was 27 years old and people knew he could drive. Hyde, however, was 30 years older. His biggest success had come more than a decade earlier. In 1969, Bobby Isaac and Hyde did win the Daytona 500, along with 16 other races, but five of those victories came on dirt tracks, and 15 came on tracks a half-mile or small-er. By 1982, those tracks were no longer on the circuit. Hyde, frankly, didn't know if an opportunity to win races might ever come his way again.

Richmond, on the other hand, was sure to get another chance. It came immediately after the Rockingham race, when things once again began to wobble with Stacy's team. Ruttman had finished third in the Daytona 500 and had qualified on the outside pole at Rockingham for his fourth top-10 start in five races. But he didn't like what he saw around him on the team, so he resigned to take over in the RahMoc car that Balough, who would eventually serve nearly four years in prison on drug charges stemming from the probe announced that February, had been driving.

So in many ways, things had come full circle. Balough was out because of the same legal issues that had done in the team Richmond was to have started the season with. When Ruttman went to take Balough's place, that opened up the seat in the No. 2 Buick owned by Stacy. And even though Ruttman's departure was another sign that things might not be quite all right with that team, it was an operation just more than one season removed from win-ning a championship. Many of the elements of that title team were gone, for sure, but its cars still offered a definite upgrade in the level of equipment to which Richmond had been accustomed.

He was more than ready to try to take advantage of it.

CHAPTER 6

Tim Richmond, Bill Elliott, Rusty Wallace, Ricky Rudd, Terry Labonte and Dale Jarrett were all born between June 1955 and November 1956. Richmond was from Ohio, Elliott from Georgia, Wallace from Missouri, Rudd from Virginia and Jarrett from North Carolina.

Labonte was the first to get to victory lane in NASCAR's top series, winning the 1980 Southern 500 at Darlington. Nearly four months shy of his 25th birthday, that ranks Labonte eighth on the all-time list of youngest winners in Cup competition.

In 1982, Wallace was still racing primarily in the Midwest in U.S. Auto Club and American Speed Association stock car events, while Jarrett was still trying to slug his way off the short tracks and start what would be a late-blooming Cup career. But Richmond, Rudd and Elliott were all beginning to establish themselves as threats to join Labonte on the list of winners on the sport's top circuit.

"Everybody kind of figured that they were going to start winning races," Chip Williams said. "But the focus of that was, at the

time, more on Rudd and Elliott. Tim would have been third on that
list and, frankly, there were probably some people who didn't necessarily want him to win. I don't think anybody really had anything
against him, but paying your dues was really big in the sport and
some people felt like he hadn't paid his."

Elliott's father, George, was a car dealer in northern Georgia,
and he had bankrolled a team that featured Bill as driver with
brothers Ernie and Dan joining him in working on the cars. The
Elliotts had been coming to the track on a limited schedule since
1976, and by the start of 1982, Bill had run 65 races. Even though
they were spending Daddy's money the same way people thought
Richmond was, the Elliotts had been around long enough and had
worked hard enough that they'd earned respect. And because they
were about as Southern as they could have possibly been, the cul-
tural barrier was never in their path.

Rudd's father, Al, had brought him to NASCAR, too, at the
tender age of 18. Rudd ran Al Rudd-owned cars until 1979, when he
spent a season in cars owned by beloved Virginian Junie Donlavey.
By 1981, Rudd had made it to DiGard, a big-time team that had won
25 races in six seasons with Darrell Waltrip as its driver. Waltrip
left DiGard after 1980 to drive for Junior Johnson, where he would
win 43 races and three championships over the next seven years—
including back-to-back titles in 1981 and 1982 where he won 12
races each year.

In 1981, Rudd finished in the top five 14 times and won three
poles. He still hadn't made it to victory lane, though, and had to
watch at Daytona as Bobby Allison opened 1982 by winning the
Daytona 500 in the DiGard car he'd been in for only one year. Rudd
had moved to the No. 3 Pontiacs owned by Richard Childress
Racing, and fell out early in four of the season's first six races, finishing no better than 15th.

At least Rudd had a ride.

Until he got to Darlington, S.C., in early April, Richmond did-n't even have that. But when Ruttman bailed out of J.D. Stacy's car, Richmond stepped in. The first time out, at Darlington, Richmond started 13th and finished fifth, a career-best finish to that point. He also led one lap, the first he'd led in Cup competition. Richmond finished 11th at North Wilkesboro, then led 18 more laps before going out with a failed oil pump just past the halfway mark at Martinsville, where he wound up 18th. He then strung together top-10 finishes in three straight races—sevenths at Talladega and Nashville and ninth at Dover—before a crash at Charlotte just 44 laps into a 400-lap race left him 40th.

While all of that was going on, turmoil swirled within the Stacy racing empire. When Sauter finished 33rd at Darlington, he was fired and replaced by Robin McCall, an 18-year-old woman who had never been in a Cup race. McCall would make two starts, in both Michigan races that year, but Stacy soon began laying off employees while others left because they starting worrying about whether they were going to get paid. Some of the five teams he was sponsoring also found themselves going to the mailbox day after day waiting on checks to arrive.

At Pocono on June 6, Richmond gave himself a chance to win for the first time. He dueled with Bobby Allison for much of the day in the Van Scoy Diamond Mine 500, and led for nine laps. Rain is often a factor in races at Pocono, and on this Sunday it began falling with the race past its halfway point. That meant that if the weather prevented the race from resuming, the leader at the time the race was called would be the winner. When the caution came out as the rain began, Allison elected to gamble that there would be no more racing, so he stayed on the track without making a pit stop for fuel.

But NASCAR kept the cars running under the yellow and when Allison ran out of fuel on the other side of the track from pit road, he had seemingly lost the race. But Dave Marcis pulled up

behind Allison's Buick and pushed it back around the track to pit
road. Allison got fuel and returned to the track without losing a lap.
When the race resumed, he eventually got by Richmond and went
on to win.

Richmond, finishing on the lead lap for the first time in his
Cup career, was second. Stacy was livid. The Chevrolet that
Marcis was driving was one of the five cars that Stacy sponsored,
and Stacy believed that Marcis's largesse toward Allison had prevented Richmond from getting his first victory. Earlier that season
at Richmond, Marcis had correctly guessed that rain would short-
en a race and stayed out to pick up a victory, making him the only
Stacy-backed driver to make it to victory lane to that point. But
Stacy didn't care. He announced that he was pulling his sponsorship because Marcis had run unauthorized associate sponsorship
decals on his car.

The next race was at Riverside on June 13, the Budweiser 400,
on a 2.62-mile road course. Richmond's talents had always seemed
uniquely tailored for success there, but he'd never had a car that
could hold up to the aggressive style with which he attacked the
course. NASCAR was primarily an oval track series, and the people who built the cars knew how to make them go fast around those
tracks. Road course racing was another discipline, and when the
circuit went to Riverside, all but a few teams did the best they
could before going back to doing what they knew how to do.

But Dale Inman, Richmond's crew chief, knew how to win at
Riverside. He'd done it with Richard Petty five times, having
worked as Petty's crew chief up until a few days after they'd won
the 1981 Daytona 500 together. Inman left the Petty team to go to
work with Earnhardt at Osterlund's team, and had hung around
through all that'd happened since.

The Budweiser 400 was a 400-kilometer race. That translated
to 248.9 miles, or 95 laps around the course about 70 miles east of
Los Angeles—20 miles or so from the site of the present-day

California Speedway in Fontana. Allison led 15 laps in the DiGard Chevrolet before losing an engine. Labonte, in a Stacy-sponsored No. 44 Buick owned by Billy Hagan, led 64 laps. But on lap 85, Labonte had to make a pit stop to top off the fuel in his tank. He came back on the track with the lead, but on lap 87 Labonte got too high in Turn 9 and lost ground.

Richmond kept coming, and on the 90th lap he swept by Labonte in a short chute between turns 6 and 8 to take the lead. Richmond pulled away over the final laps, winning by 3.82 seconds.

In just his ninth start with the Stacy team, and his 43rd career NASCAR Winston Cup race overall, he had won for the first time.

"My initial feeling is, 'Let's go out and win the next one.' I'm high on the win. I don't know what to say," Richmond said after the victory, for which his team earned $21,530. "I'm not surprised I won as soon as I did. I cut a tire down at Darlington and lost a lap there. We had one of the fastest cars in the field and maybe we could have won. I think we could have won at Martinsville, too. We should have won at Pocono last week. I'm a bit surprised we hadn't won before now."

That was Tim Richmond.

Just more than two months earlier at Darlington, he'd finished on the lead lap for the first time in his career. His car at Martinsville had lasted barely halfway through a 500-lap race. At Pocono, Allison had led 75 laps to Richmond's nine. But Richmond believed—and it was not merely bravado—that he could have, and perhaps should have, won those races.

This, too, was Tim Richmond.

A few years later, when asked to reflect back on that first career victory, the thing Richmond remembered most was not the joy of victory lane.

"When you take the checkered flag there, you slow down and have time to see the whole crowd again," Richmond said. There were about 45,000 people at Riverside that day, and as he took his victory lap he was drinking in their cheers. "I drove slowly and looked at the fans and saw happy gestures. And then I looked in the back straight and a guy was hanging over the fence. I waved and he was yelling at me with his thumbs down."

As Richmond passed, the disgruntled fan—one guy in a crowd of 45,000—changed the gesture from a down-turned thumb to an upturned middle finger.

"That one guy took the polish off of everything," Richmond said. "I really considered stopping the car, going over and asking what the problem was, why he felt that way toward me. God, did that hurt."

The hunger for approval and affection that made the memory Richmond harbored from his first victory speaks volumes about what would happen to NASCAR's newest winner over the next few years. The date on which it happened, June 13, would also one day hold particular significance.

But in the immediate aftermath of the win at Riverside, there was joy in the Stacy camp. Or at least there should have been. Stacy had told Marcis on race day that he was pulling his sponsorship, and after Parsons finished 23rd at Riverside, Stacy pressured his team's owner, Harry Ranier, to fire Parsons, who was fourth in points after having eight top-10 finishes in the first 14 races. Ranier did so, replacing him with Buddy Baker. Later that week, Stacy took the additional step of ending his sponsorship of Labonte's car with Hagan's team—while Labonte was leading the points standings! Stacy claimed Labonte's uniform carried an "unauthorized" sponsor's patch, but the patch in question was for a company owned by Hagan, the car's owner.

Clearly, the true motivation behind Stacy's decision to pull his sponsorships was financial. Once again, he'd sold more than he could deliver. Later in the year, Ranier took Stacy's logos off his car and said he would sue to get money he was owed. Jack Beebe, who owned Bouchard's car, eventually did the same.

By late fall, Stacy had only Richmond's cars and sponsorship of driver Jody Ridley's cars owned by Donlavey. Equipment was being spirited away from Richmond's team's shop at night out of fear it might be repossessed or that the shop would be locked up and the gear impounded because of the building legal battles.

Richmond finished outside the top 20 in six of the eight races following the win at Riverside, crashing out twice and failing to finish three times because of mechanical issues. He did finish fifth at Nashville and seventh at Talladega, and at Bristol in August won his first career pole with a speed of 112.507 mph around the .533-mile track. He led 81 laps in the race but blew an engine.

Richmond started seventh the next weekend, in the Southern 500 at Darlington, a race that wound up being a terrific battle among Cale Yarborough, Richard Petty, Dale Earnhardt and Bill Elliott. Yarborough, driving the No. 27 Buick owned by M.C. Anderson, and Petty went at it particularly hard as they fought for the lead.

"The crowd hadn't sat down all day," said Harold Elliott, then the engine-builder for Yarborough's team. "Cale and Richard were racing side by side all day, but all of a sudden while they were doing it, this car comes along and passes them both. Tim had been a lap down, and he just drove right by them. I asked Barry (Dodson), 'Who was that?' He said Tim Richmond. I guess I hadn't been paying any attention to him, but I started that day."

Dodson had been watching Richmond ever since the day he first saw the driver wearing the Evel Knievel suit.

"You could tell he was a natural," Dodson said. "My father drove most of his life, but had to quit racing because he had eight kids to raise. He worked as a superintendent in a quarry and it came down to racing or his job, and he took the job because he figured it would always be there. Dad said to me that he thought Tim was a modern-day Curtis Turner. The best three natural drivers he'd ever seen were Turner, Tim and Cale."

Yarborough outdueled Petty and came away with the victory, his fifth career win in the Southern 500. But as soon as the race was over, trouble struck the winner's team. The victory was the third for Yarborough in a season in which he ran only 16 races. He'd won three straight championships from 1976 to 1978 while driving for Junior Johnson, but he had left that team after those three titles and 41 race wins in six years, because he had reached a point where he no longer wanted to run a full schedule. Tim Brewer felt likewise. He'd been crew chief for Yarborough in the 1978 championship sea- son and had stayed with Johnson's team through Waltrip's first title there in 1981. But he'd joined Anderson's team for 1982 because, in part, of its part-time approach.

Anderson, though, wanted a championship of his own. His team had finished fifth in the standings in 1979 and third in 1980 with Parsons as its driver. He now had a driver and a crew chief who had both been champions and saw no reason not to go after the 1983 crown.

"M.C. wanted to run for a championship, but Cale didn't," Dodson said. "Brewer and Harold Elliott didn't either. They'd pret- ty much found a gravy train running 16 races a year and still making really good money. They kept giving M.C. all of these reasons why we shouldn't race for the championship. M.C. wanted to know why we couldn't—we'd come close with Benny Parsons. I knew M.C. well enough, he was one of the best men I ever worked for, and he wasn't asking for too much."

Indeed, Anderson had decided that if his team didn't want to go for a championship, he would simply shut the doors and get out of the sport. And after Yarborough's victory in the Southern 500, Anderson told a reporter that's exactly what he was planning to do after the final three races the team was scheduled to run that year.

"M.C. came up to me and said, 'Well Brewer, I'm quitting,'" Brewer said. "I said, 'What?!'"

As the shock of that decision rippled through the sport, Richmond finished second at Richmond and ninth at Dover in the two races after Darlington. With Stacy's racing operation crumbling around him, though, he was also looking ahead to 1983. One person he'd talked to was Raymond Beadle, the drag racer who Richmond had known through his friend Fred Miller.

"He wanted to know if I would go NASCAR racing," Beadle said. "We talked about it, but we didn't have anything but an idea. We started working on it, looking for a sponsor. I was doing pretty well in drag racing and I put out a few feelers."

Beadle had worked before with Max Muhleman, who owned a marketing company in Charlotte that had connections in the motorsports industry. Muhleman set up a meeting for Beadle in Milwaukee with representatives from Miller Beer. Brewer, meanwhile, knew Beadle and got wind of his possible interest in becoming a NASCAR team owner. "M.C. Anderson had offered to sell Harold Elliott and I the whole program for $250,000," Brewer said. "Harold and I had just started to make a little bit of money, and $250,000 was a ton of money. I called Raymond and I said, 'Hoss, you've been wanting to buy a Winston Cup team? Here's your chance.'"

As Richmond finished out the season with Stacy's team, he and Beadle were also working on their deal to purchase Anderson's team and go racing in 1983. They'd set up shop at a hotel near the airport in Atlanta, which at that time was the hub for all air travel in the Southeast. At the meeting in Milwaukee, the Miller officials said they'd heard that Yarborough was also working on a deal to buy the equipment from Anderson. They didn't want to agree to support Beadle's team if Beadle didn't actually wind up having a team.

So Beadle flew back to Atlanta, and he and Richmond then flew to Savannah to wrap up the purchase of the team. "We thought we'd have Miller for sure," Beadle said. "We flew back to Charlotte, though, and found out they hadn't decided." The beer company was also talking to DiGard about replacing Gatorade as the sponsor on Bobby Allison's cars. Coors, another beer sponsor, was looking at NASCAR, too, but it would not be until 1984 before it decided to jump in to sponsor Bill Elliott's cars that were now owned by Harry Melling.

"We had spent all of this money and now we didn't have a sponsor," Beadle said. "We also didn't have a shop, and all of our cars were in Savannah."

Beadle was also still trying to line up the key people to help build cars in which Richmond could go fast. When Anderson announced he was shutting down his team, other teams began calling Harold Elliott to see if he'd come build engines for them. Elliott was talking most intently to Petty Enterprises, considering an offer to go to the team's operation in Level Cross, N.C., to help Richard Petty and Kyle Petty keep adding to the family's long list of NASCAR success.

On the final Sunday of the 1982 season, the Cup circuit was back in Southern California for the Winston Western 500 at Riverside.

"We didn't go to Riverside, so I was sitting at my father-in-law's house in North Carolina watching the race that day," Harold Elliott said. "Raymond Beadle called me and asked me if I'd made my mind up what I was going to do.

"He asked me, 'Are you watching the race?'" Elliott said. "I said yes, and he said, 'Who's leading?'"

Richmond was dominating the field on his way to completing a Riverside sweep for the season. He would wind up leading 92 of 119 laps, winning by 7.85 seconds over Rudd to complete a season in which he'd had seven top-five and 12 top-10 finishes in 26 starts, winning $175,980 and finishing 14th in the final standings despite having missed four races.

"That's who's going to be our driver," Beadle told Elliott.

Early the next week, Elliott called Dale Inman and asked Inman what he thought of Richmond. "I said, 'Is he any good?'" Elliott said. "Inman said, 'Yes, he's good, but you've got to calm him down just about every lap.'"

Elliott made up his mind. When he called to tell Kyle Petty he wouldn't be coming to that team, Petty asked why. I told him I was going to work with Raymond and Tim Richmond," Elliott said. "Kyle said, 'All Tim will do is tear up race cars.'"

All Elliott could see, though, was Darlington, where he'd seen Richmond pass Yarborough and Petty as they fought for the lead in the Southern 500. The axiom in racing is that it's easier to teach a driver to slow down than it is to teach him how to mash the gas.

Elliott, Dodson, Brewer and Beadle would soon find out, however, that Richmond would give that accepted wisdom a run for its money.

CHAPTER 7

The story of how the name of a medal given to German ace fighter pilots from World War I became the name for the NASCAR Winston Cup team that Tim Richmond drove with from 1983 to 1985 starts with a drag racer named Harry Schmidt.

Schmidt had named his drag racing team after the Blue Max medal, given to German pilots who scored 20 or more "kills" in action in World War I and was popularized in a 1966 movie called *The Blue Max*. By the mid-1970s, however, Schmidt was ready to get out of drag racing. Raymond Beadle was not, but he seemed to be headed that way, too, when Don Schumacher decided to shut down the three-car team for which Beadle had raced.

Beadle called Schmidt and talked him into being his chief mechanic near the end of his final season with Schumacher 1974. The next year, the Blue Max funny car was back on the track with Schmidt turning the wrenches and Beadle behind the wheel. Beadle enjoyed the very parts of the business that Schmidt hadn't liked—driving, promotions and the business end of drag racing. Beadle quickly trademarked the name, incorporated the medal into the paint scheme and started lining up merchandise, sponsors and race dates.

The National Hot Rod Association's most important event each year is the U.S. Nationals on Labor Day weekend in Indianapolis. Going into the 1975 Nationals, Don "The Snake" Prudhomme had won every funny car final except one during the season. Prudhomme also had been five for five when reaching the elimination final at the U.S. Nationals, but Beadle ran a 6.16- second quarter-mile in the final to back up an earlier 6.14 run, giving him the NHRA elapsed time record as well as a victory, by a tenth of a second, over Prudhomme.

By 1977, Beadle had bought out Schmidt's interest in the Blue Max team. Dale Emery, himself a former funny car driver, and Fred Miller, Richmond's boyhood friend from Ashland, Ohio, worked on the cars. All three would eventually be named to the NHRA Hall of Fame. With their team based in Dallas, Texas, Beadle won NHRA funny car championships in 1979, 1980 and 1981. He also won the 1981 funny car title in the rival International Hot Rod Association, becoming just the second man to win those titles in the same year. He also became the first IHRA driver to break the six-second barrier in a funny car with a 5.99 elapsed time at Rockingham Dragway in North Carolina.

So when Beadle, who in 2001 would be selected as the 20th best driver all-time as the NHRA, celebrating its 50th anniversary, went looking for a sponsor for his racing operations for the 1982 season, he was a hot property. His plan was to package his drag racing team with the NASCAR team and a World of Outlaws sprint-car team for Sammy Swindell under the Blue Max banner.

After failing to land the Miller sponsorship, and with Coors still sitting on the sidelines, Beadle next turned to the Stroh's Brewery, based in Detroit. "We needed to hurry and get the deal done," Beadle said. "Finally, on December 23, we got it signed."

Tim Brewer, still stewing a bit over the fact that he'd just built a nice house on the Intracoastal Waterway near Savannah, where he thought he'd be living while running a partial schedule with M.C. Anderson's team, was instead trying to secure a shop for the new Blue Max stock car team in the Charlotte area. He and Harold Elliott were also in charge of getting the team's cars and equipment moved to the new headquarters in a space they wound up leasing from Billy Hagan in time for the team to prepare for the 1983 Daytona 500.

"The Wednesday after Tim had won the last race of 1982 at Riverside, he and Raymond Beadle flew down to see what they'd bought," Elliott said. "I went up to the airport to pick them up. Raymond and I went into the airport and were sitting there having a beer. I guess Tim was taking care of the fuel bill for the plane or something, but in a little while he came in and sat down. That was the first time I met him. He didn't say a whole lot, but we were talking about what kind of cars we were going to run. Tim pulled out a picture of the Pontiac and said they'd worked things out with Stroh's and Pontiac."

Brewer got the final word from Beadle that Stroh's was on board. Richmond's cars would carry the No. 27 and be sponsored by Old Milwaukee beer, one of the Stroh's Brewery's brands.

While Brewer and Elliott came to Blue Max, some of the old gang from M.C. Anderson's team went with Yarborough to Harry Ranier's team—Barry Dodson, Pete Peterson and Eddie Craft.

Brewer thought about joining them.

"Harry Ranier called me and asked if I'd come over there and interview," Brewer said. "I went over and talked to Waddell Wilson, and he was having a good run and we were both making pretty good money. He wanted to hire me, but when we started talking money it turned out to be a dead end."

The original plan was for Richmond to drive a Pontiac Grand Prix. "We started with the Grand Prix and went to Daytona to test," Brewer said. "I was not a fan of the Grand Prix. We did all of the things we were supposed to do in the tests, but we just could not get the Grand Prix to run. So we went back and got a Pontiac LeMans, and that's what we wound up building for Tim. It accented his driving style to no end."

When the teams assembled in Daytona for the season's first race, Richmond had a competitive car.

"We had a fast, fast car," Elliott said. "Tim pulled out to try to make a pass for the lead in his 125-mile qualifying race, and the motor just shut off. We tore that motor apart and couldn't find anything wrong with it. I always thought they were running so fast that when he pulled out from behind the other car the air just blew right past the cowl and the engine shut off because no air was coming into it."

Richmond started 24th in the race and again felt like he had a good car. But just 24 laps into Blue Max Racing's first NASCAR Cup points event, the timing gear came loose and the engine failed. Richmond finished 41st.

"NASCAR wouldn't let us have a lot of rear spoiler for the LeMans," Brewer said. "We struggled at some places early on, but gradually we got it figured out and matched it to Tim's way of driving."

At Darlington in the season's fifth race, Richmond ran 157.818 mph to win his first pole for Blue Max.

Brewer still laughs about that day.

"I will never forget that," he said. "Tim ran his lap and Darrell Waltrip was timing it with a stopwatch. Tim came across the line and Darrell just threw his stopwatch down and said, 'There ain't no way in hell anybody can run around here that fast.' They forgot to tell that to old Slim," using his nickname for Richmond.

Tom Higgins remembers that lap, too.

"I saw him come off the old Turn 4 completely sideways," Higgins said. The track has since been reconfigured; with the start-finish line moved to the other side so that what was Turn 4 is now Turn 2. "The thought that raced through my mind was, 'This is going to be one hell of a wreck.' But he kept control of it and won the pole. As far as being a natural, having that seat-of-your-pants control, he was right up there with Curtis Turner and Junior Johnson. And that is up there, that's the stratosphere."

On race day, however, the mood in the Richmond pits changed in a hurry.

"When they dropped the green flag, Tim took off so hard going into Turn 1," Brewer said. "He had everybody by several car lengths coming off the second turn, but he forgot to take it out of third gear. He blew the motor up, and we took out Terry Labonte and several other guys."

Two races later, at Martinsville, Richmond led 58 laps and was in contention to win until his team put left-side tires, which were softer and therefore provided more grip, on the right side of his car. That was against NASCAR rules, whether the team did it on purpose or by accident, and when officials noticed it they ordered Richmond to come in to serve a five-lap penalty. He finished 15th.

When an oil line broke after 65 laps at Riverside in early June, in a race in which Ricky Rudd finally got his first career win, it left Richmond with a 28th-place finish at a track where he'd won twice the previous year, had started on the front row and led eight laps that day. It also was the seventh time in 13 races that Richmond had not been running when the race ended. To that point, he had just four top-10 finishes and was 19th in the points.

It was time to shake things up.

"Brewer called me up," Barry Dodson said. "Tim's car had been fast at times, but they were struggling. They had the ingredients over there, but they just weren't making soup."

Dodson had been working for Ranier's team, where Yarborough had stormed out of the gate by winning the Daytona 500 and again at Atlanta in his third race of the 1983 season. Brewer wanted him to come to Blue Max and bring the rest of the old gang along, too.

Dodson couldn't resist, and after the disappointment at Riverside, the tide began to turn. Richmond ran fourth at Pocono and third at Michigan. Ignition woes did him in at Daytona, where he finished 31st, but he was third at Nashville before heading back to Pocono for the Like Cola 500 on July 24.

"We had gone to Pocono to test," Elliott said. "I knew about Indy cars and I knew how important the shocks were to how one of those cars felt under the driver. Tim knew how he wanted a car to feel. We'd drive to one auto parts store and buy shocks and come back and try them for a while, then we'd go somewhere else and buy more. We spent three days doing that, working on hardly anything else."

When the team went back, Richmond was confident his car was ready to roll.

"We couldn't get him to practice," Dodson said. "He went out and rode around one time and then he came in."

Joe Mattioli had grown more and more fond of Richmond since first talking him into coming to his track three years earlier. He knew that Richmond loved the Polish sausages served at the track's concession stands, so he brought a couple over for Richmond's lunch.

"He sat on the trunk of the car eating those things," Dodson said. "We were telling him that he needed to go out and run some laps. He said, 'I don't need to run, I know what I've got.' But he'd run only about a 63-second lap. I said, 'Tim, you need to go run. Terry Labonte just ran a 60.25.' Tim said, 'I don't care what he ran.'"

Finally, Elliott convinced Richmond to go out and run a lap, then cut off the engine quickly so Elliott could check the spark plugs. "Tim half-assed a lap at 62-something and came in and said he was ready," Dodson said. "We were worried to death in one sense, but on the other hand we weren't because we knew who we were dealing with."

Richmond had drawn a late number in the qualifying order, which each week is determined at random. That could be an advantage, since cooler weather later in the day usually meant faster track. But on this qualifying day in July, the difference in temperature was going to be negligible.

"Harry Gant was on the pole at something like 59.75 seconds," Dodson said. "Travis Carter was his crew chief and he was sitting on the pit wall. Tim Brewer was sitting beside Travis and I was sitting beside Brewer. Travis looked at Brewer and said, 'When Richmond comes by, I am going to hit my stopwatch. If he runs what I think he might, the next thing I am going to hit is you.' Tim went by and ran 59.25. He pulled in and got out, just like that."

Richmond's lap speed of 151.918 mph had won him the pole. Earlier in the week, he'd told friends that he had a feeling deep in his gut that it was going to be a good weekend.

Sunday certainly wound up being a long day.

Pocono Raceway sits on a flat spot in the mountains of Pennsylvania. Before Mattioli and his wife, Rose, put a race track there, most of the land it sits on was used to grow spinach. The fact that farming was done there was no coincidence, either, because the geography and weather patterns ensure plenty of rain. On July 24, 1983, it rained twice. Thirty-four laps into the Like Cola 500, the field was stopped for nearly 40 minutes waiting out a shower. After a caution on lap 134, rain came again and caused another delay of more than an hour.

Eleven different drivers would lead that day, swapping the top spot 41 times. Just before the second rain delay hit, Richmond passed Darrell Waltrip to take over the lead. Moments later, just as the rain began, Greg Sacks smacked the wall in Turn 1 to bring out a yellow flag that was followed shortly thereafter by the red.

The Blue Max team decided to leave Richmond on the track without stopping for fuel as long as they could, thinking the rain might not go away and the race would be called. But when the rain stopped, NASCAR put the cars back on the track so the heat they generated riding around under the yellow flag would help complete the track-drying process. Richmond had to pit for fuel on lap 145.

When the green finally came back out on lap 154, just before 6:30 p.m., Bobby Allison was in front. Gant took the lead away on lap 160, and then Waltrip led lap 161. Richmond then came up and led the next three laps. Gant passed Richmond and led five laps, but Richmond came back and led the next five. Waltrip then took over from lap 175 until he had to pit for a splash of fuel on lap 188, giving the lead back to Richmond. When Richmond stopped for fuel, Bill Elliott took the lead. Elliott stopped on lap 193 and Dave Marcis led a lap, but Richmond passed him on lap 194 and led the final seven laps.

"We were watching the weather," Richmond said afterward. "We took a chance. The track was still a little wet after the green. We were hoping we'd get the win under the caution and with the rain, but I am glad it happened like this. The fans got what they paid for."

Over the remainder of their first season together, the Blue Max team began to grow closer. They had grown more and more convinced that their driver had uncanny natural abilities, and began to understand that it would be their jobs to build cars that could not only show that, but could withstand the all-out aggressiveness Richmond brought with him to the track.

"You could not impress on him enough that he had to back off the gas pedal at some point in time," Brewer said. "He wanted to go into the corner at 200 mph, then he wanted the car to just turn in the middle and come off the turn straight. I told him, 'Good luck finding somebody who can build you that car, pal.'"

Fred Miller said that Richmond knew how to do one thing better than anybody he's ever seen.

"He would absolutely stand on that gas pedal, I promise you," Miller said. "The one thing he lacked that would have put him so far ahead of everybody else was the thing that Rusty Wallace had when he came in, that mechanical ability. Tim couldn't get out of the car and say, 'We need to put in this shock,' or 'We need to adjust it this much.' But he stood on the gas, and if it was right he was going to run good. And if it wasn't, he was going into the wall, because he was not going to let off of it."

That pattern held up absolutely through the remainder of the 1983 season. In the 12 races that followed his victory at Pocono, Richmond finished in the top five six times and was 10th once. In the other five races, he either crashed out or parked early because of engine problems.

He didn't win again that year, but he came close twice.

At Rockingham, he and Terry Labonte staged one of the great battles in that track's history, racing nose to tail when they weren't side by side in the waning laps. Richmond gave Labonte everything he had, but Labonte held on to win by seventh-tenths of a second.

Two races later, the season would wrap up at Riverside, a place where Richmond was already regarded as a virtuoso by many in the sport.

"You would be surprised at the number of people who would come to me at Riverside to find out where we drew for qualifying," Brewer said. "They wanted to make sure their cars were ready so they could go out and watch Tim come through the 'esses' there."

Brewer had worked with Waltrip at Junior Johnson's team, and he knew that Richmond's emerging popularity and flamboyance rubbed Waltrip the wrong way—Waltrip didn't need any competition for the spotlight he'd been basking in for years.

"Tim would make Darrell so mad he couldn't see straight," Brewer said. "A couple of times at Riverside, Darrell would be qualifying behind us. I'd tell Tim to run off the track on his cooldown lap and kick some dirt and rocks up onto the track because Darrell was next. Darrell would just come in raising hell."

Dodson said Richmond's style in attacking the Riverside course could best be summed up in one word.

"He would just sashay around there," Dodson said. "Before that last race in 1983, Darrell came up to Tim and said, 'I know you're going to pass me up there in Turn 6, because you're the only person here who can make that move. When you pass me, go ahead and don't beat and bang on my car. Just pass me and go on.' Tim just laughed."

Brewer remembers that race vividly.

"We were leading and it was raining cats and dogs," Brewer said. "We were sitting in the transporter waiting on them to call the race." But NASCAR chief technical inspector Bill Gazaway came and told the team the race was about to resume.

"I told him it was still wet, but Bill said we were going to restart it," Brewer said. "I said, 'Is it because we're leading?'"

Richmond led 31 laps in the Winston Western 500. Waltrip, trying to catch Bobby Allison in the battle for the championship, led 34 laps as well, but late in the race their cars got together in Turn 9 and spun off the track. "Darrell pretty much wrecked us," Dodson said. Both cars recovered, with Richmond finishing fifth and Waltrip sixth.

"After the race was over, Jeff Hammond was getting ready to kick the side of my car," Brewer said. Hammond was now Waltrip's crew chief. "Pete Peterson grabbed him. We were getting ready to have a hell of a fight that day."

Bill Elliott won that race, scoring his first career victory, while Allison finished ninth to hold off Waltrip by 47 points for the championship.

For a brand-new team, Blue Max had done well. The win at Pocono was the highlight, of course, and Richmond also had nine other top-five finishes. Late in the season, he'd won poles at Charlotte and Atlanta, giving him four for the year. Only Waltrip, who won seven poles, had more. In the 17 races in which his car was running at the finish, he was in the top 10 in 15 of those. And to have failed to finish 13 times, his 10th-place finish in the final standings was respectable, too.

Moreover, Richmond had begun to shed the "outsider" label that had followed him to the South. He was living in the Charlotte area, and he was racing with a team that included guys who had always been part of the NASCAR fraternity.

"That team had Barry Dodson and Harold Elliott and Pete Peterson and guys like that who everybody in the sport knew and were buddies with," Chip Williams said. "Those guys were telling people, 'Hey, this Richmond kid is really OK.' That paved the way for Tim somewhat. It made people give Tim a second look."

Another image of Richmond, however, was emerging.

When the season ended, he was 28 years old. When he wanted to, he could put on the costume that everybody else in the sport wore to the track—perhaps his blue jeans would have a little sharper crease, though. But he also cleaned up extremely well.

"A lot of guys are what people would call handsome," Buddy Baker joked many years later. "I'll be danged if Tim Richmond wasn't almost pretty."

Williams saw Richmond's appeal emerging.

"Richmond was the first driver I saw who really appealed to women and to younger guys at the same time," Williams said. "From the young guy's standpoint, it was an identification thing. He was like them. There weren't many guys then who were flashy and out front and successful. There were some cool guys who weren't all that successful, and there were successful guys who weren't all that cool. Tim was among the first who was both."

The party was just starting.

CHAPTER 8

In many ways, Tim Richmond was a stranger in his own era.

"He would have thrived in the late 1950s and the 1960s," Tom Higgins said. "He would have had legions of fans because he had the same style that Curtis Turner and those guys did—just full bore and run it until the wheels fell off. And in today's NASCAR, what a driver needs to be is articulate and good-looking, somebody who has the ability to make a good public impression. Tim was way ahead of his time on that."

The all-out, hammer-down style was part of NASCAR's early years, when many of its drivers "trained" by running dark, winding back roads across the Southeast hauling illegal whiskey and dodging the local law and the federal revenue agents who were looking for them.

While men like Junior Johnson hauled "moonshine," Turner and Weatherly were the ring leaders of a group in the 1960s that seemed determined to drink as much whiskey as a whole fleet of 'shine runners could tote. Turner raced every bit as hard as he partied, and that means Turner was one of the hardest racers who ever lived. He was also, in the minds of many, one of the best to ever drive in NASCAR.

By 1984, as Richmond started his second season with the Blue Max team, stories about the way he played off the track were beginning to make the rounds. As with many of the legends about Turner, the question lingers about how many of them were actually true.

At the same time, Richmond was also years ahead of his time in many ways.

"Tim was the first guy in NASCAR to wear a full-faced helmet," Barry Dodson said. "He wore a fire-retardant sock over his head under the helmet, and everybody laughed at him. Twenty years later, everybody finally figured out a full-faced helmet made sense. And pretty soon, they're all going to be smart enough to wear fire socks."

Richmond brought those safety features with him from Indy car racing, where the alcohol-based fuel burns without visible flames and can be deadly. He also helped spread another element of Indy racing to stock cars—the use of a motor home as a place of refuge for himself, his family and his team during race weekends.

"In 1983, Tim was telling everybody we needed to have motor homes at the track so we could entertain potential sponsors and help the sport grow," Dodson said. "Everybody laughed at that, too." Today, the infield at a NASCAR Nextel Cup race track looks like a massive lot where luxury recreational vehicles are sold. Not only does virtually every driver stay in one these days, so do most car owners, crew chiefs and even a few television announcers.

"He was just a time traveler, stuck in the wrong place," Kyle Petty said. "He could have raced against my grandfather and been right at home in those days. And today, he wouldn't stick out at all. Jeff Gordon has a place to stay when he goes to New York? Tim beat him there by about 25 years. NASCAR has an office in Los Angeles because it wants to be a factor in Hollywood? Tim beat them there by 20 years.

"When you look at it, he was going every place that NASCAR would eventually go. Whether that was just because of his personality and his marketability, or whether he had the foresight to see what was coming, whichever it was, he was way out ahead of everyone. And his racing backed up what he was doing."

If there was a kindred spirit for racing in NASCAR in the mid-1980s, it most likely was H.A. "Humpy" Wheeler, the president of Charlotte Motor Speedway.

Stock car racing's answer to P.T. Barnum, Wheeler had worked his way up from running a dirt track in Gastonia, N.C., a town about 20 miles west of Charlotte in the same county as Belmont, the town where Wheeler had grown up while his father worked as athletic director at a small Catholic college, Belmont Abbey.

Wheeler had worked in various jobs in racing for years, including a key role in Firestone's racing tire program. When the 1.5-mile Charlotte track was first built, he helped get it up and running for his old friend Bruton Smith—who'd originally partnered with Curtis Turner in getting it built. Construction delays and cost overruns had put the track in serious financial trouble shortly after it held its first race, the 1960 World 600, and Smith eventually lost control of the track. Wheeler left when the banks took over, but after Smith came back in the early 1970s to regain controlling interest in the track, he hired Wheeler again in 1975, and he's been there since.

Wheeler was born to promote. He's held mock invasions and circuses on his track's infield before NASCAR races. He's had a daredevil jumping over cars in a school bus. He had a swimmer break the world's record for treading water during one of his race weekends, but his plan to assemble the world's largest marching band went sour when that race day came up with unseasonably warm temperatures and band members standing on the hot pavement in their wool uniforms started wilting by the dozens.

One other thing that Richmond and Wheeler shared was a temper.

The entry blank for the 1983 Miller High Life 500 at Charlotte Motor Speedway listed the award for winning the pole for that race at $32,000—a significant sum since first place in the race itself would pay just over $40,000. The prize, the entry blank said, would include $17,000 in cash and a 1983 Ford Thunderbird Turbo Coupe valued at $15,000.

"All week, he was telling me he wanted that Thunderbird," Brewer said. "My deal with Raymond Beadle at the time was that when we won a pole, Harold Elliott and I got 50 percent of that money. So I told Tim he could have the car and Harold and I would take the cash."

On Thursday, Richmond won the pole with a lap at 163.073 mph. But when Wheeler presented Richmond with the car he'd won, Richmond was incensed. "Some public relations person from the track had been driving the car," Brewer said. "It had about 15,000 miles on it and had cigarette burns on the upholstery and all of that."

Wheeler chuckles about what transpired today. But in 1983, he wasn't laughing.

"It was serious," he said. "Tim wanted a new car and what we were giving away was one of the pace cars we'd driven around town to various places promoting the race. That was the car we were giving him."

Wheeler, who grew up boxing in amateur competition and continued to box while he was in college at South Carolina, was in no mood to hear Richmond's complaints. And Richmond was of no mind to back down. There was what some witnesses described as a brief "shoving match," with Wheeler doing most of the shoving before he left the garage. As you can imagine, the incident caused a stir.

"The next day, Tim comes into the truck and says, 'Brewer, you've got to give me some of that money,'" Brewer said. "I said, 'For what?' He said, 'For winning the pole!' He started complaining about the car and I said, 'Hey, Humpy's the one who gave you that car. You wanted it and that's what you've got. We've already spent the money.'"

Richmond and Wheeler went into Wheeler's office for a "meeting" that lasted nearly an hour. Nobody really knew what to expect when the two hotheads emerged, but they managed to surprise everybody.

"The next thing I know, here come Humpy and Tim walking through the garage area and they start pretending like they're wrestling with each other," Brewer said. "A crowd gathers around them and they've got ketchup all over themselves like they've been bleeding and they're carrying boxing gloves around their necks. That was Humpy just putting on a big show, and Richmond was right in there with him."

When the 1984 season opened, Richmond started 10th in the Daytona 500 but lost an engine after just 66 laps and finished 33rd. It was not a good omen. He ran seventh at Richmond, but crashed out at Rockingham and lost a valve at Atlanta, finishing poorly both times. After a fifth at Bristol, though, the Blue Max team finally stitched together a good run at North Wilkesboro.

"We had struggled all day to run fourth or fifth," Brewer said. "But a caution came out with about 30 laps to go and I told him, 'You put that thing in third gear and come down pit road just as fast as that thing will run.' He shot in there and we slapped four tires on it and got him back out."

Richmond's pit stall was near the exit of the pit lane and he didn't have far to go to beat everyone back onto the track. He got out first and led the final 28 laps, beating Harry Gant by 3.59 seconds. Ricky Rudd, who had led 290 laps, finished third. Darrell Waltrip, who'd won the past five races at the North Wilkesboro track that his car owner—and Brewer's former employer—Junior Johnson called home, was sixth.

Richmond's first career short-track win provided only a momentary respite, however. He went out early with crashes or mechanical issues in each of the next four races, meaning he'd failed to finish seven times in his first 10 races.

But Richmond then ran well at Dover, chasing Richard Petty all day on his way to a second-place finish. After a 10th at Charlotte, he contended at Riverside, too, but had to come in for a late pit stop after making contact while racing with eventual winner Terry Labonte and wound up sixth. When he finished fifth at Pocono, the team had strung together four top-10 finishes and had begun to feel a little better about things.

Even when things weren't going particularly well on the race track, however, the Blue Max team was on top of other aspects of its game.

"We didn't lose any parties," Dodson said. "Never.

"We'd get to town and check into the hotel and find the bar. We'd sit there and drink a few beers and just see what happened. When everybody on the team decided to turn in, we'd turn in. If the garage opened at 6 a.m., that might be 4:30 a.m. or it might be midnight. I don't know of a place we went to that we didn't have a good time.

"Old Milwaukee was our sponsor, and they'd take us out for some kind of function and say, 'We're going to do this as a team.' We'd be there an hour or two and they'd say, 'That's all the beer.' I guess we would exceed their budget. We'd say, 'Do you want us to start drinking Miller?' And if they cut us off, that's what we did.

"We closed down some bars and we got into some fights, but we were just typical racers. We were like Butch Cassidy and the

Sundance Kid. Some guys on other teams would be going to bed the night before at 9 or 10 o'clock, and we'd come into the garage the next day feeling horrible and go faster than they did. They'd be like, 'Who are these guys? What are they made of? How are they doing this?' We did it feeling terrible, but the only way to feel better was to go right back the next night and do it again."

It was an era in the sport that's much different from today's corporate-driven NASCAR, Kyle Petty said.

"Everybody still stayed at hotels and every hotel had a bar and a restaurant," Petty said. "Depending on which hotel you and your team stayed at, you had your own world away from the track. You might be at the same hotel with three or four other teams and you'd see them every night, but you wouldn't see anybody else from another team.

"And you also can't talk about how Tim Richmond was unless you put him in context with the culture in our country in the mid-1980s. Go back and look at what was on television back then."

In 1984, the top-rated television show in America was the prime-time soap opera *Dynasty*. For the previous four years, it had been *Dallas*. In 1985, *Miami Vice* debuted and set a fashion tone for much of the country.

"Television is a reflection of society, and shows like *Dallas* and *Miami Vice* were all about excess and who could make the most money. You had good guys and bad guys, but the good guys seemed to be the losers and the bad guys were getting farther and farther ahead. Who was making money on Wall Street? The corporate raiders. It was all about the art of the deal. It was all about excess.

"We'd been through the war- and protest-torn 1960s and spent the 1970s laid back trying to heal from all of that. The 1980s were all about trying to catch back up to where we might have been if things had kept on rocking since the 1950s. When you're trying to make up for lost time, you go overboard.

"In a lot of ways, Tim was part Hollywood, part *Miami Vice* and part New York City come to NASCAR. He liked fast cars, he liked having a boat, he liked the Hollywood look. He'd go to New York and go to Studio 54 and ride around in a limo. He was different from Richard Petty and Darrell Waltrip, and that made people notice him."

Another thing set Richmond apart, too. While most of his fellow Cup drivers were married, Richmond was not.

"Just about everybody else had a wife and kids," Petty said. "Stories about him being with all of these good-looking women would be passed along from one crew member to the next and from one fan to another fan. Some of it almost became urban legend. Some of his reputation was deserved . . . but you have to remember that a lot of guys were thinking, 'That's how I would be acting if I were single and I looked like him.'"

Fred Miller had a set of keys to Richmond's house on Lake Norman, and when the Blue Max drag-racing team needed a place to light when its travels brought it through the Carolinas, that's where they set up shop.

"Tim wound up getting a bad rap," Miller said. "Don't get me wrong, we partied hard in those days. But everybody did. If I ever decided to write a book about some of the things I saw, a lot of racers would want to have me bumped off. We all rocked and rolled pretty good.

"But a lot of what people said about Tim was bull. He didn't drink any more than the rest of us. And yes, there were drugs around in those days and people were doing them. Was Tim a drug addict? No!

"Did he chase women? He didn't have to. When he moved to Lake Norman there wasn't but one store up there. We'd go to the store and come back to his house. While we were unloading the groceries, the doorbell would ring. Two or three girls had followed him home. You know what? At his age, he was single and good-looking. If he hadn't let people see him with a lot of women around him, you know what people would have been saying about him—they would have said he was gay.

"Was he a wild man? No, but he was always the life of the party. The party followed Tim around. He liked having a good time, and he wasn't the kind of person who kept to himself.

"My nickname was 'Waterbed Fred,' OK? There was a reason Tim and I hit it off. Both of us, when we walked into the room people just noticed us. He didn't set out to be the center of attention, but that's what he was."

Many of the people who were closest to Richmond say that the "playboy" image that grew around him was simply one of the roles the driver with aspirations of being a movie star played.

"Tim laughed about it," said Sandy Welsh, his half-sister, about the image. "He didn't try to dispel it. Yes, he had a good time, but not to the extent that people blew it out of proportion.'

The image, at the very least, certainly did not paint a complete picture.

"We saw a different side of Tim, the family side," Welsh said. "He loved to cook, and he wanted to buy this little restaurant called the Evergreen that's still there in Ashland. He had his own recipe that he marinated chicken in and grilled it. He wanted to buy that restaurant and sell people cold beer and grilled chicken and have a patio for them to sit on. He was buying things like little cement flamingoes and sculptures as he traveled around. He was collecting them for that restaurant."

Harold Elliott remembers one party at Richmond's Lake Norman house in 1983.

"My wife was pregnant," Elliott said. "He was going to cook for us that night, and he also loved to refurbish old barber chairs. He'd restored one with blue velvet and he sat it right in the middle of his living room. He waited on her hand and foot that night.

"People always said Tim was the life of the party, but you know what? Life was a party for him, and he wanted everybody to have a good time. I don't think there's a damn thing wrong with that."

Dodson said he and Richmond had a motto.

"Short time here, long time gone," Dodson said. "Every day is Saturday. That's what we said. And we didn't take any prisoners. We got to the track and unloaded and expected to win the pole and win the race—or crash. And normally, we did. If we wanted to stay out all night, we did that, too.

"But there was a side of Tim that most people didn't see. He was so good to my kids. He was great with children. He was just good with everybody, whether you were eight or 80 it didn't matter. He could fit in with people in Hollywood and New York, but one year after we qualified at Talladega, we got in the rental car and rode around the infield where all of the race fans were. We'd get out and party with them.

"He had no enemies. I don't know of anybody who didn't like him. I do know some people who were envious and jealous of him because of his abilities—and not just his ability to drive a race car. He had the ability to be a genuine human being."

Jerry Punch remembered hearing about a limousine ride that was taking Richmond and Dale Earnhardt to an appearance.

"There were about a half-mile from the track and passed this poor guy wearing a racing cap and carrying his cooler, just walking down the road either on his way home or to his car somewhere," Punch said. "They went by and Tim told the limo driver to turn around. He was adamant. They fought the traffic to come back the other way toward the track and picked the guy up."

And then there was the man at Dover.

"Tim had been out late one night up there," Dodson said. "He was going into this little diner to get something to eat and he saw this guy outside. He asked Tim for some money or to buy him something to eat."

Richmond didn't merely reach into his pocket and pull off a few bills. He invited the man inside to have dinner with him.

"The guy said he had hadn't had anything to eat in two or three days," Dodson said. "Tim whispered to the waitress to bring them both T-bone steaks—steak and eggs. When they brought the food to the table, though, the guy started crying. He didn't have any teeth, so he couldn't eat the steak. So Tim ordered him four sandwiches and took him home.

"The guy lived in a trailer somewhere and he had nothing. Nothing. The next day after practice, Tim went out and bought a hot plate and took it to him. As best as I know, every time we went back to Dover after that, Tim went to see that man and took him things. That's the side of Tim Richmond that a lot of people never saw and nobody ever talks about."

CHAPTER 9

By the middle of the 1984 season, the Blue Max team had become a close-knit group. They knew they had a driver who could win races if they could just keep a car underneath him, and they also had all but perfected the art of having a good time.

At the July race in Daytona, Richmond started back in 41st but worked his way up to an 11th-place finish. But as the race wound down, Richmond and David Pearson began to get crossways with one another.

"They got to beating on each other's fenders," Tim Brewer said. "Under the yellow flag, Tim stuck his middle finger up at Pearson. He called me over the radio and said, 'You guys need to come down here, I think me and Pearson are getting ready to fight.'

"Raymond (Beadle) asked me what Tim said. I said, 'He said David Pearson is getting ready to whip his ass.'

When the race ended, the cars headed for the garage area while Brewer and the crew hurried back from pit road to try to keep their driver from getting into trouble with Pearson, the sport's second all-time winningest driver, who was 50 years old at the time.

"I got down there and came around the corner and saw Tim getting up off the ground. Tim had smarted off to Pearson, and Pearson just kind of slapped Tim a little bit. I walked up with Beadle and Tim had a handprint on the side of his face. Tim said, 'Pearson hit me!'

"I said, 'Did you stick your finger up at him?' Tim nodded. I said, 'I told you to leave those old guys alone! He slapped you. If Pearson had hit you, you'd be over there passed out right now.'"

Today, the summer race at Daytona is held on Saturday evening under lights at the 2.5-mile track. In 1984, the Firecracker 400 was still being held on July 4 and began in the late morning. Many drivers and crew members would finish the race and then spend the late afternoon on the white sand of Daytona Beach.

Brewer's son, Scott, was still a toddler at the time. On the afternoon after the incident with Pearson, Richmond came to the motel where Brewer and his family were staying and went down to the beach with them.

"He just started playing in the sand with Scott and was having the best time," Brewer remembered. "I asked him, 'Hey, Slim, have you ever thought about hanging with a younger crowd?'"

Most of the Blue Max team made it back home to North Carolina by late that evening. The next day, a Thursday, was a big day.

"We went over to somebody's house on the lake to have our Firecracker 400 party," Dodson said. "At 7 that morning Todd Parrott jumped off the roof of the house with a green flag to start the party."

Parrott, the son of legendary crew chief Buddy Parrott, is now crew chief for Elliott Sadler's No. 38 Fords on the NASCAR Nextel Cup circuit. He won a championship in 1999 with Dale Jarrett.

"Yep," Parrott said when asked if Dodson's recollection was accurate. "Boy, was that a party."

Richmond came to the party in his speedboat, cruising over from his house on the lake about dusk with one of his buddies. They'd already been "limbering up" for the festivities, so when Richmond got out of the boat instead of tying it off to the dock, he tied a rope from the front end of the boat to the back end.

"It had just about got good and dark and somebody's kid, maybe from next door or something, came up and said there was a boat going out across the water," Dodson said. "We looked but it was so dark we didn't see anything. The music was going and there were girls everywhere, so it wasn't like we looked all that hard.

"Sometime that night the last person standing, and I don't know who that was, fell off the house with the checkered flag to end the party. We all just kind of crashed over there, and the next morning when Tim got up he was freaking out. His boat was gone!

"I thought back to that little boy had said, so we got in somebody's boat and we hunted and hunted and hunted. We finally found it on the other side of the lake. It had drifted all the way across the lake and somehow backed itself right into somebody's slip just perfect. The rope was still tied to the back of the boat. After we found it, it was hilarious. We laughed about that for years, but that's just way things went for us."

The party, it seemed, wound up being wherever Richmond was.

"One time after a race at Michigan, we were staying over because on Monday we were all supposed to go the Stroh's Brewery and then go to a Detroit Tigers game," Harold Elliott said. "Sunday night after the race, we went into Detroit and checked into the hotel and we went out, in our uniforms, and stayed out to about 3 a.m. Tim took us to a couple of places that were really dives, places that guys like us had no business being in. I mean, these places had cement blocks on the floor with a door laid across them, and that was the bar.

"One place, I told Tim, 'We're going to get killed in here. We're the only white people in this joint and these people don't know who you are.' Tim said, 'That's why I like it here.' We paid a cab driver about $200 to haul us around all night.

"Tim just wanted to be with us, around people. He could not stand to be by himself. He'd do what we wanted to do, we'd go bowling or we'd go the movies. We did a lot of things, but the only thing people seem to want to remember is the party part of it. Heck, if I had been Tim Richmond in those days, been single and young and good-looking, there's no way I could have controlled myself as good as he did."

Chip Williams said NASCAR officials heard tales about Richmond and the Blue Max team and their exploits away from the track, but that nothing about those stories raised many eyebrows.

"You'd hear that they had been out partying and playing, but in those days everybody was partying and playing," Williams said. "The parties were good in those days, but they were not as great as they've become in everybody's memories. A lot of people came to the track in the mornings without having had much sleep the night before. It was going on, but Tim was just partying with other people in the sport. It really wasn't a big deal."

Another big difference was the nature of the sport. In 1984, NASCAR simply was not as big of a deal on the American sports scene as it is today.

"We just were not as image-conscious as we are today," Williams said. "We didn't have to worry about the *National Enquirer* picking up stories about our drivers and running them. The *New York Times* didn't care. Heck, *The Charlotte Observer* wasn't even covering every race. There wasn't as much to worry about."

Darrell Waltrip, who after finishing his remarkable career as a driver moved into the Fox Sports broadcasting booth when NASCAR got its first national network television contract before the 2001 season, has been credited with coming up with the most succinct way of describing the difference between the sport then and the sport now. "We used to have wine for dinner," Waltrip said. "Now we have it with dinner."

The seeds of that change were first beginning to be sown in 1984, however.

Richard Petty had left his family's team and signed to drive for car owner Mike Curb for the 1984 season. When Petty won at Dover, it was the 199th of his career.

Then at Daytona, when Brewer was trying to keep Richmond from having Pearson rearrange his face after the Firecracker 400, Petty was celebrating his 200th career victory alongside President Ronald Reagan. Reagan had given the command for the field to fire its engines from Air Force One on the way to Florida, and then watched the end of the race from the tower where NASCAR officials supervised the race.

The president's presence at Petty's milestone victory was a huge shot of publicity for NASCAR at a time when the sport was picking up a bit of momentum toward expanding from its regional base.

ESPN, then in just its fifth year of existence but already becoming a staple of cable television around the country, was beginning to turn to NASCAR as well as other forms of auto racing to provide programming for its 24-hour broadcast day. And people in the sport were beginning to understand that for NASCAR to grow, it needed sponsors from outside the traditional categories like motor oil and engine additives.

By 1984, Budweiser, Coors and Old Milwaukee were all sponsoring cars. Wrangler was selling blue jeans off two cars, driven by Dale Earnhardt and Ricky Rudd. Hardee's, a chain of fast-food restaurants, was on Cale Yarborough's car and Kyle Petty, the only car running out of the Petty Enterprises shop, carried the No. 7 and was backed by 7-Eleven convenience stores.

The winds of change were beginning to rustle things at Blue Max Racing, as well. Throughout the summer and fall of the 1984 season, the team had not been able to put things together well enough to contend for victories.

Richmond's No. 27 Pontiac finished ninth at Pocono, then ran into another stretch of bad luck with three crashes and two engine failures in an eight-race span. The only bright spot in that stretch came in the Southern 500, where Richmond finished second behind Harry Gant's dominant Chevrolet—Gant led 277 of 367 laps in the race, while Richmond led only one lap.

Gant's car was still owned by Hal Needham, the film director whose movie, *Stroker Ace*, had come out the previous year. Earlier that year, Needham had approached Brewer with an idea for a second team that was to have included Richmond.

"Hal came to me at Michigan and asked me if he started a second team would I run it for him," Brewer said. "I told him I'd talk to him because Beadle owed me and Harold Elliott some money. Hal said he and Burt Reynolds were going to put a deal together for Richmond and had some people to fund it. But nothing ever came of it."

There had been other hooks in the water, too. Toward the end of 1983, when Richmond was winding up his first year with Blue Max, he also talked to a Charlotte car dealer named Rick Hendrick who was starting a new NASCAR Cup team. At one point, Hendrick thought he had a deal done with Richard Petty to drive the car, but when that fell through he talked to Richmond and Geoffrey Bodine. Richmond actually had a contract in hand, and if he had signed it he would have been the Hendrick team's first driver. But Richmond couldn't make himself pull the plug at Blue Max after just one year. Bodine wound up with the Hendrick ride, pairing with crew chief Harry Hyde, who was trying to make one more comeback.

It took Bodine and Hyde just eight races to give the new team, then called All-Star Racing, its first Cup victory at Martinsville. Bodine also won at Nashville and then concluded 1984 by winning at Riverside, with Richmond finishing second.

Richmond's early season win at North Wilkesboro, five other top-five finishes and a total of 11 top 10s helped him finish 12th in the standings. Once again, he had fallen out before the end of too many races—12—to do much better in the points, and he hadn't won a pole after having won four the previous year.

Despite the feelers from elsewhere, Richmond would be back at Blue Max for 1985. Brewer, however, would not. He left the team to return to work for Junior Johnson, taking over as crew chief on the cars driven by Neil Bonnett. Dodson stayed on, and the team brought in Jimmy Makar, who would later win a championship as a crew chief in 2000 with Bobby Labonte.

Even when things are going well, auto racing can be a frustrating pursuit. In a great season, a driver may win 20 percent of the races he enters. When Jeff Gordon put together three remarkable years in 1996-98, winning 33 races in that span, he still lost 63 times.

It is frustrating for a driver who believes he has the ability to run competitively to not be able to keep up because his equipment is just not good enough. It's even more maddening, however, for a driver to know he and his team are capable of winning because they've done it, but for some reason can't find the way back to victory lane.

As the 1985 season began, Dodson knew Blue Max should have done better than it had in 1984. One reason was he knew what his driver could do in a race car.

"One time we were at Riverside and he hung his goggles up on the mirror while he was riding around under the caution," Dodson said. "The race started back and he realized he didn't have them on. He took the green in Turn 8 and came down the back into Turn 9.

He was going under the bridge and running about 180 mph there. He was driving with his knees and reaching up to get his goggles before Turn 9. He could do things that you're not supposed to be able to do in a race car."

Richmond was also still incredibly competitive, the same as he was when he'd have his father time him running to and from the mailbox at their home in Ashland when he was just a lad.

"If you went out and played golf with him, he was going to beat you," Dodson said. "If you shot pool with him, he was going to beat you. If you went bowling with him, he was going to beat you. He always did it with a happy-go-lucky kind of attitude, but he was that competitive."

Richmond never professed to be otherwise.

"I have no reservations about saying that I am more competitive than anybody out there," he said in a magazine interview done that year. "I have more drive to win than anybody out there. Period. Not just as much, more. I am here to win and so is everybody else. But I'm here to do it more than everybody else. That's my attitude."

That didn't mean Richmond lacked a mischievous side.

"The funniest thing that happened when Tim was with us was at Daytona for the Fourth of July race there in 1985," Dodson said. "We were running terrible that year, and that was our fault and not his. Anyway, NASCAR had Bill Gazaway in the control tower back then and we could hear him on the scanner. I heard Bill say, 'He needs to move up or we're going to bring him in before the start.' I didn't know what they were talking about. This was on the parade lap. They were saying 'Tell the 27 to get into position.'

"I asked Tim what was going on. He said, 'Nothing, man. This is great.' You can't see anything from pit road at Daytona, so everybody comes through the trioval and we're not in line where we're supposed to be. Tim's about 100 yards behind the field holding an American flag out the window.

"He came by the pit, and keyed the mike. 'Look boys,' he said, 'it's America's birthday!' They were so mad at him they almost didn't let him start the race."

But Richmond said the "good-time Charlie" image bothered him at times.

"It's amazing how much people can talk about things they don't know," Richmond said. "If they could only talk about things they do know as much as they do about things they don't, I guess they wouldn't be talking as much.

"My attitude now is give the people the opportunity to get to know me, and then whatever they decipher out of that, well, so be it. I can't change anything, and I'm not going to go out of my way to do anything about it. It would be more constructive for me not to worry about what people are thinking than try to change their minds. I am better off trying to make good impressions on the people who don't think anything yet. I'm not worried about what people think now, not as much as I used to be.

"I would give anything if I could just step out of myself and take off, get my little cooler, my blanket and my six pack and go up in the grandstands and just sit there. . . . And just watch. I would like to observe myself and see how people form their images of me. Then I might have a different story. I might even change some of the things I do. I really don't know how people form their opinions of me."

Once again in 1985, Richmond didn't get his season off to a great start at Daytona. He started 33rd in the 500 and finished 35th, crashing after 66 laps on a day when Bill Elliott won and began to write a story that pushed NASCAR up one more notch in notoriety.

R.J. Reynolds Tobacco, the company behind Winston's sponsorship of the NASCAR Cup circuit, was offering a $1 million bonus that year to any driver who could win three of the sport's four most significant races—the Daytona 500, the Winston 500 at

Talladega, the Coca-Cola World 600 at Charlotte and the Southern 500 at Darlington. When Elliott won at Talladega, he gave himself two chances to pick up the $1 million bonus. How big of a deal was a $1 million prize in 1985? The total purse for the Daytona 500, for all 40 cars that made the race, was just $1,097,925.

While Elliott was stacking up victories, winning nine times in the season's first 18 races, Richmond was struggling. He did string together five straight top-10 finishes through the June race at Michigan, but the best thing he'd done all year to that point was win in the Busch Series for the first time in his career that May in Charlotte in the No. 15 Pontiac owned by Rick Hendrick in which Earnhardt had won the same race two years earlier.

Richmond and Earnhardt had become fast friends.

"I was out on Lake Norman fishing with this friend of mine one day," Tom Higgins said. "We were busting up the lake in this rocket of a bass boat this guy had, and we met this boat that was going even faster than we were. The guy driving that boat waved at us and we turned around and pulled up beside them. It was Dale and his wife, Teresa, with Tim and one of his girlfriends."

One of Richmond's favorite stories about his friendship with Earnhardt also involved a day on the lake. The two were water-skiing, taking turns driving the boat and towing the other behind. They had with them a jar of "Cherry Bounce," moonshine made by one of their racing buddies who still delved in that traditional craft.

The driver of the boat would take a cherry that had been in the jar, soaking up the alcohol, and toss it into the air. The object was for the skier to catch it out of the air and eat it. According to Richmond, Earnhardt's aim was particularly good, because he ate so many spiked cherries that day he nearly drowned.

"I think Earnhardt grew to respect Tim because when they were in the race car, you didn't see Tim's leather coat or his long hair," Jerry Punch said. "All you could see was the race car and what the man who was driving it was doing. Earnhardt could see that Richmond's car was tight or loose or whatever. All he knew was this guy kept rolling up alongside of him. He made Earnhardt drive hard, and when you made Earnhardt get up on the steering wheel, you had done something."

Sandy Welsh saw her half-brother's friendship with Earnhardt growing, too.

"Tim would say he and Dale would get bored out there and start messing with each other, because the fans liked it," Welsh said. "They had fun. At Michigan one time, we were in the motor home and Dale and Tim and had raced in some kind of demolition derby at an appearance. Both of them got banged up. Tim was on the couch and Earnhardt came in to see how he was. They talked a little bit and agreed it was that stupidest thing they'd ever done and that they'd never do it again."

At Bristol in August of 1985, Earnhardt had controlled much of the race until a miscue on pit road with just more than 50 laps remaining handed Richmond the lead. Earnhardt tried several times to get back around his friend and rival, then finally resorted the classic short-track tactic of the "bump-and-run." Earnhardt put his front bumper to the rear end of Richmond's Pontiac and nudged it out of the way. He then made the pass for the lead and went on to win with Richmond finishing second.

Elliott was the big story the next week. He'd failed to win at Charlotte in May, so he came to Darlington for the Southern 500 with the $1 million bonus back on the line. Elliott, who'd won at Darlington earlier in the year and in the race before Earnhardt's Bristol win had also completed a season's sweep at Michigan, battled his way past a feisty Cale Yarborough and won the race and the $1 million, putting NASCAR on the cover of *Sports Illustrated* magazine and giving it the kind of attention it so rarely got in that era.

Earnhardt and Richmond tangled again later in the season at Martinsville, where Richmond had perhaps his best car of the year.

"He overdrove it in qualifying and you can't do that at Martinsville," Dodson said. "We qualified 17th, but we told him on Saturday that we were as fast as anybody and that we could win the race from a pit stall on the backstretch, as hard as that was to do."

He led 159 laps, but Earnhardt chased him down, and the two went at it, banging sheet metal as they raced side by side through traffic battling for the lead. Earnhardt tried to boot Richmond out of the way again, but Richmond turned left and delivered a shot of his own. They were still trading paint when Richmond had to back off to avoid a car spinning in front of him in his lane. Earnhardt kept going and took the lead.

"We had to come in and last pit like everybody else," Dodson said. "A lug nut got caught between the wheel and the brake caliper, and when he left the right front wheel locked up. He went around Turns 1 and 2 and the tire blew out."

Richmond finished seventh, and he was ticked off at Earnhardt, who held on to win. "I owe him one," Richmond said.

Richmond strung together another stretch of five top-10 finishes in a row that fall, from Dover to Rockingham. But as his third season with Blue Max came to a close, it was clear to everyone their time together was over. Richmond and Beadle were squabbling here and there over money, and nobody was happy with the season—three top-five finishes, 13 top 10s and an 11th-place finish in the points.

Over at Rick Hendrick's team, now called Hendrick Motorsports, Bodine had also gone without a victory in the 1985 season. What's more, Bodine and Hyde were not getting along. At all. But that was OK. As long as Hendrick could keep them from wringing each other's necks over the final weeks of the 1985 season, which at times seemed like it would be impossible to pull off, he had a plan.

Tim Richmond was a big part of it.

CHAPTER 10

Rick Hendrick started out just looking for a place to store the boats he no longer had the heart to take racing.

"When Jimmy Wright got killed in one of my boats, I just couldn't do it any more," Hendrick said. "Richard Broome worked with us on the boat program and he knew Harry Hyde. Richard told me we could store the boats we had at Harry's shop. I rode over there with Richard one day and that's when I met Harry. I'd heard of him, of course, but I'd never met him."

Hyde's shop was located just up the hill from a trailer where he lived, on a piece of property in Harrisburg, N.C., barely a mile from the Charlotte Motor Speedway.

"Everybody thought Harry was washed up, that the sport had passed him by," Hendrick said. "He was old school, but he was like a diamond and people just didn't know it. They knew what a character he was, but Harry had tremendous knowledge about how to run a car and make it survive a race. He built a car like a tank with a lot of extra coolers and brakes. He was that kind of guy. He was different from a lot of people even back in that time. He always took care of your money.

"Harry had this great line about that. He said, 'If a guy has a lot of money and wants to get into racing, he needs to find a crew chief with experience. In five years, the crew chief will have the money and owner will have the experience.' A lot of guys went broke who, if they had met Harry Hyde, they would have been OK."

Hendrick walked around Hyde's shop and saw the old pictures of Hyde and Bobby Isaac from the Nord Krauskopf days. Since the debacle with J.D. Stacy, Hyde had picked up work in NASCAR here and there but never had found anything substantial. He had not, however, lost his desire to race. He told Hendrick that if he could just get another chance with a decent team, he knew he could build cars that could win. Hendrick made his living selling cars, but Hyde was selling Hendrick on the idea of starting a NASCAR Cup team.

Hyde's cajoling turned out to be well-timed, too, because within a matter of a days, Max Muhleman—the same marketing expert in Charlotte who'd helped Raymond Beadle set up his deal that started the Blue Max team—came to Hendrick with an opportunity. C.K. Spurlock, who owned the Gambler Chassis Company, was looking to get into NASCAR. Spurlock was working with country music singer Kenny Rogers, whose song *The Gambler* had been a huge hit in 1979. The idea was to get Hendrick as the car owner, with Spurlock and Rogers helping to line up sponsorship. The driver they wanted was Richard Petty, so that the "King" of stock-car racing and the reigning "King" of country music would be working together.

All in all, it was a nice, neat marketing plan. None of it ever happened.

"When we got to Daytona in 1984, we didn't have Richard Petty, we didn't have Kenny Rogers and we didn't have a sponsor," Hendrick said. What he did have was Hyde, making $500 a week, as crew chief; Geoff Bodine, a driver from Chemung, N.Y., who'd been in cars owned by Cliff Stewart for the previous two seasons; and too much pride to quit.

"I was in pretty deep," Hendrick said. "I felt like I'd made an announcement to the world. I was nervous and scared, but once I got into it and saw it and got around it, I thought, 'We can do this.' I had a tremendous amount of respect for Harry, and Bodine drove the wheels off the car."

The car was a Chevrolet that Hyde built for Hendrick. Bodine started ninth in the team's first race, the Daytona 500, and finished eighth, and added top-10 finishes in his next two starts as well. As Hendrick was trying to convince Northwestern Security Life Insurance to sign on to sponsor the team, Bodine won at Martinsville in its eighth race. The sponsor signed, and All-Star Racing was on its way.

Three poles and three wins helped produce the team's ninth-place points finish, and Hendrick signed Levi Garrett, a brand of chewing tobacco, as his new sponsor for 1985. Bodine won three more poles, all in a four-race stretch late in the season, and led more laps than he had the year before when he won three times, but the No. 5 Chevrolet never made it to victory lane that year.

"If you go back and look, we should have won almost every race," Hendrick said. "But I am an old drag racer and I wanted to make as much power as we could. We wanted to be as fast as, or faster than all the other guys, but we hadn't had the learning curve yet to find out where the weak links were in the chain. We had no relationship with anybody else to help us, so we were kind of learning as we went. But we had the darn power. We just had to learn how to make it better."

Bodine and Hyde, Hendrick said, were a good pairing—at first.

"You had two hungry guys, one of them trying to get a start and the other trying to get reborn," Hendrick said. "They got together

and wanted it so bad they did well. But then they got a little success and started arguing over who should get the credit."

Hyde was every bit the "old school" racer that Hendrick
believed he was. Bodine, though, had his own ideas about racing
and race cars. His father owned the Chemung Speedrome in his
hometown in New York, and Bodine had started racing micro-
midget cars there when he was five. He once won 55 races in a
modified car in one season and was NASCAR Cup rookie of the
year in 1982. Two of his brothers, Todd and Brett, would follow him
into NASCAR competition. Geoffrey still ran in several Cup races
in the 2004 season at 55 years old after surviving one of the scariest
on-track accidents in NASCAR history in a NASCAR Craftsman
Truck Series race at Daytona in 2000.

Bodine helped introduce power steering to NASCAR during
his career, so he certainly had his own ideas about how to build
and set up a race car. Eventually, some of those ideas began to con-
flict with Hyde's.

"Things were changing in the sport, and I was trying to show
him some of those changes," Bodine said. "Harry liked to put a lot
of weight in the back of his cars. Some places that worked. When
we won at Martinsville, he had a ton of lead weight in the back of
the car. I tried to explain to him that it worked like a pendulum.
You put that weight back there and go into the corner, it just
swings the back end of the car out. He said, "Bodine, I don't know
about no pendulum. This is a race car.'"

Hendrick was growing weary of playing referee.

"Geoff would say and do some of the dumbest things,"
Hendrick said. "He is really a good guy, but he'd just do or say the
wrong thing. Harry, at the same time, when he got against you or
got his mind made up, you weren't going to change it."

During the 1985 season, as Bodine and Hyde struggled at
Hendrick and Richmond couldn't get untracked at Blue Max,

Hendrick began talking to Procter & Gamble, one of the largest consumer product companies in the world, about sponsoring a second team through its Folgers coffee brand.

"Folgers came to me and said, 'We want to start a team, and we would like you to run it,'" Hendrick said. "They thought my deal with Levi Garrett was for one year, but it was a multiyear deal. I told them I could start a second team and they agreed with that. I was kind of a young guy coming from a marketing side of racing instead of the mechanical side, but our team proved that first year it could win."

After Hendrick found out in late 1983 that Richard Petty wasn't going to be his driver, he had first offered a contract to Richmond to drive for him in 1984. He was talking with Bodine, too, and Richmond kept waffling on his decision. Finally, Hendrick gave Richmond at deadline. At 4 p.m. on that day, Hendrick had to have an answer. At 10 that morning, Bodine came to Hendrick's office at City Chevrolet in Charlotte. When Hendrick told Bodine he'd given Richmond until 4 p.m. to sign, Bodine said he understood, and then asked Hendrick if it would be OK if he just waited at the dealership in case Richmond called back with his decision. Bodine stayed for several hours, and that impressed Hendrick. He eventually tracked Richmond down and said he had decided that Bodine would be his driver.

At the same time, Hendrick still had his eye on Richmond.

"I saw in Tim Richmond a lot of what I would later see in Jeff Gordon," Hendrick said. "Tim could drive a car that was so out of shape and do it every lap. . . . I really thought Tim could do it. He tore up a lot of stuff, but I really thought he could drive. When we did the deal with Bodine and that car started running good, that year Tim immediately started talking to me. He said, 'I would really like to do that deal.'"

There were common threads to their stories. Like Richmond, some people in racing initially resented Hendrick for the money behind his foray into racing. When Hendrick's team won in just its eighth start, the whole issue of paying one's dues came up again.

Now, just a little more than a year into his tenure as a car owner, Hendrick was about to add a second team. Today in NASCAR, single-car teams are virtually extinct. In the mid-1980s, however, it was hard to find anybody beyond Junior Johnson who believed a two-car team would work in NASCAR Winston Cup— and Johnson was having his own troubles getting his two-car team with Darrell Waltrip and Neil Bonnett as his drivers clicking on all cylinders.

"The Folgers people said, 'We want you to own our car,'" Hendrick said. "I said, 'Well, I want to hire Tim Richmond to drive it.' They said, 'No, no way.' They didn't want him in their car as wild as he was supposed to be. I said, 'Look, he can drive the car. I will handle him.' We met some more and they asked me if I really thought I could handle him. I told them I knew I could."

Hendrick had also reached an agreement with Gary Nelson to be his second crew chief. By September 1985 he had things in place. All Hendrick had to do the rest of that year was keep Hyde and Bodine from choking each other.

"They were just fighting like crazy," said Hendrick, whose plan was to put Nelson with Bodine on the No. 5 team and pair Hyde and Richmond on the new No. 25 car. "I had a meeting with Harry and Geoff and the team, and I said, 'Look, we have eight races left. To be sure, we can get through eight races.' We had two sponsors; life was going to be good. We just had to get through eight races without killing each other and blowing up the sponsor deals."

Hendrick and the team talked for nearly two hours. Then Bodine stood up.

"I can do that," he said. "I know we can get to the end, we'll do that and make it work."

Now, it was Hyde's turn.

Tim Richmond as a boy.

As a youngster, Tim competed in quarter horse shows and won dozens of trophies and ribbons.

Tim Richmond's high school graduation portrait from Miami Military Academy.

The famous post-race ride from the 1980 Indianapolis 500. Tim Richmond hitches a ride on the sidepod of racewinner Johnny Rutherford's car after Richmond's car stopped on the track at the end of the race.

Tim's eighth career start on February 22, 1981 at Richmond, Virginia, in the UNO car just before the race.

April 26, 1981 at Martinsville. It is Tim's 14th career Winston Cup start and he finishes 14th. Here Tim is shown running just behind Richard Petty.

This was taken at Indianapolis Raceway Park before the 1983 Busch race. Tim had taped the speakers from his radio to his ears with silver duct tape.

PHOTO COURTESY OF DICK CONWAY

PHOTO COURTESY OF DICK CONWAY

Tim buckles his chin strap prior to the 1983 IRP Busch race. You can see the fire in his eyes.

Movie director Hal Needham (far left) explains a scene from the forgettable movie *Stroker Ace* in which Richmond (shown in Stacy driver's suit) had a small role. In working on that movie, Tim's interest in acting was kindled.

Ricky Rudd, Tim Richmond, former NASCAR president Bill France Jr., Hal Needham, Kyle Petty and Dale Earnhardt pose before shooting a scene in *Stroker Ace*.

Tim Richmond didn't
mind showing off.

Harry Hyde, Dennis Connor, Tim Richmond,
Rick Hendrick, and Evelyn Richmond celebrate a win.

Tim is joined in victory lane by his parents, Evelyn and Al.

Tim finished 10th at the 1984 Charlotte World 600.

PHOTO COURTESY OF DICK CONWAY

Tim races side by side against his greatest rival,
Dale Earnhardt, at the 1985 Richmond Fairgrounds.

PHOTO COURTESY OF SANDY WELSH

Tim accepts the award for winning the most poles in the
1986 season at the NASCAR banquet at the Waldorf-
Astoria hotel in New York City. Only days after this photo
was taken, Richmond learned that he had AIDS.

"Bodine," Hyde said. "You are a prick, but I love Rick Hendrick enough I will make this work."

Hendrick was exasperated. "I took Harry outside," he said. "I said, 'Harry, we've been talking for two hours and you just pissed on the whole deal.'"

Hyde was unrepentant. "I told him what I thought," Hyde said of Bodine. "He IS a prick."

As Bodine and Hyde promised to make it to the end of the season, so Hendrick turned his attention to making sure he kept his promise to rein in Richmond and keep the new sponsor from getting too nervous. It was not a simple task, as Jimmy Johnson, one of Hendrick's top business lieutenants, found out the first time he met Richmond.

Johnson went to work for Hendrick in one of his car dealerships in North Carolina in 1983. Johnson was dating a woman who lived in Florida, however, so when Hendrick asked him to move to Hudson, Florida, about 60 miles from Tampa, to help run a dealership, Johnson was more than happy to do it.

When Hendrick signed Richmond in 1985, he promised to give Richmond a car from one of his dealerships to drive. Hendrick asked Johnson to get someone to deliver an IROC Camaro to the marina in Fort Lauderdale where Richmond had a houseboat. Johnson, who had already agreed to move back to North Carolina and take over as general manager of the motorsports program in time for the 1986 season, decided to handle the job himself so he could meet one of the drivers he'd be working with.

"I left about six in the morning and pulled up at the marina about nine or something like that," Johnson said. "Tim had told me what slip his houseboat was docked it. I finally found it, and it was quiet as a mouse. I was looking and I heard somebody say, 'Hey!' I looked up on the deck on the top of the boat and there was Tim in a little Speedo bathing suit. He said, 'Come on up here.' I went up there and he had maybe a six-pack of beers, empty, and a big tray full of crab legs he had already eaten."

Johnson and Richmond visited briefly, and Richmond provided a tour of the boat that the manufacturer had given him in return for being a spokesman for the company. Johnson had a 1 p.m. flight back across the state to Tampa, so he asked Richmond to drive him to the airport.

"That," Johnson said, "was a big mistake.

"We went flying down the road, this six- or eight-lane highway with like a four-inch curb separating the two sides. All of a sudden, he says, 'You want a cup of coffee?' I said I wasn't much of a coffee drinker, but he jerked the wheel to the left and we jumped the curb running 70 or 80. That thing started sliding backward into incoming traffic and he slid it around, jerked it back into low gear and floored it. We're spinning the wheels going backward. You couldn't see for the smoke. The thing took off and he went immediately back over the curb, across in front of traffic and down an embankment into the parking lot of this coffee shop."

Johnson looked at Richmond incredulously.

"I said, 'What the hell was all of that?'" Johnson said. "Tim said, 'They're topless.' We went inside, and sure enough it was a topless coffee shop because they had outlawed topless bars in Fort Lauderdale. So went in and got a cup of coffee and 'checked out the interior.'

"We got back in the car and went to the airport, where they were doing a lot of construction work there. Tim and I pulled up under the parking deck and I opened the door and I had one leg out, turning to say goodbye and that I was looking forward to working with him. But a cab pulled up behind us and the guy blew his horn. Tim looked in the mirror, put the car in reverse and stomped the gas. He drilled that cab. I almost broke my damn leg. It knocked the cab driver back and he went peeling out, and Tim jerked the car out of reverse into gear and took off after him—with me trying to get back in the car and shut the door. We chased that cab through the construction with workers scattering. The cab ran a stoplight and got away from us.

"Tim said, 'I can't stand for somebody to do that to me.' Then he took me back and dropped me off. That was my initiation to Tim."

Early the next year, as the start of the '86 season approached, Folgers sent some of its top officials and advertising representatives to Charlotte to meet with key players in the race team to plan their marketing strategies.

"It was a freezing cold day," Johnson said. "We had a meeting that was supposed to start at 9 a.m. Harry and Rick and I showed up in three-piece suits, this was our first meeting with these guys to make up the game plan and talk about what they're expecting. It was a big meeting; we wanted it to be perfect. We wanted to make a first impression.

"We started the meeting, just sort of talking, and they had concerns about Tim and his reputation. Rick was telling them, 'I've got this covered. Tim and I have a great relationship, and I promise you I am going to clean him up.'

"Tim showed up about a half-hour late. He walked in and he had on this big old fur coat and after-ski boots with fur around the tops, ugly-looking things. He took the fur coat off and threw it across the table. Under that, he had on a T-shirt that said something like "Eat More Possum" and a pair of jogging shorts that were cut up the side. Tim went and sat at the head of the table and threw his leg up on the table. Everything just fell out. Rick and Harry and I were saying, 'Oh my God!' That kind of thing never stopped."

Richmond's first public appearance for Folgers came at one of the company's plants in New Orleans. He was supposed to be at the plant at 8 a.m. Country music star T.G. Shepherd, who also was a spokesman for Folgers, was on time. So was Hyde. Richmond, however, was late. Finally someone went to his hotel and got a housekeeper to open the room. Richmond was still snoozing after having been seen in the company of two young ladies the night before in the hotel's bar. Apparently, Johnson said, the two women had slipped sleeping pills into Richmond's drink and stolen his wallet and an expensive watch before leaving.

When Richmond made it to the plant, where various state and local officials had been waiting along with everyone else, he peered out from behind dark sunglasses and said, "If Folgers coffee can wake me up, it can wake anybody up."

It was a nice save, but Hendrick was not amused. "I told him, 'Tim, you're going to have to clean yourself up,'" Hendrick said.

Richmond, it seemed, understood that—at least to some degree.

One Saturday night in late 1985, Dr. Jerry Punch was working in a hospital emergency room in Bunnell, Florida, when he was paged to take a phone call.

"It was about 9 o'clock, and it was Tim," Punch said. "He was watching the sunset out at this party in Malibu, one of those parties that he was going to by that time where there were celebrities everywhere. He told me that he needed to get his act together. He had the opportunity to drive for Rick Hendrick and said he felt like it could be the best thing that had happened to him in his career. I was starting one of those 20-hour days you get in emergency rooms and we were covered up with patients. I told Tim that if he was serious, he needed to get his behind out of Hollywood and away from those people and to get his butt back East. I said, 'If you come here and you show me that you're serious, I will help you, but first I will have to see where you are physically.'"

Punch was on duty until noon the next day.

"About 10:30 in the morning, Tim came strolling into the ER," Punch said. "He'd gotten on a red-eye flight and came walking in wearing a pair of floral shorts, a Hawaiian shirt and some sandal-like flip-flops. We talked a little bit and I did a little brief exam."

Punch and Hendrick talked and made arrangements for Richmond to go to Houston's Cooper Clinic, for fitness, diet and lifestyle training. "We knew that this kid had a lot to offer the sport," Punch said.

CHAPTER 11

The first time the racing world saw Richmond for the 1986 season, jaws dropped.

"When he came to Daytona he had on a silk suit that probably cost him $1,000 and he was carrying a cane and this little 'man purse,'" Rick Hendrick said. "He had his hair done like he had just stepped off the cover of *GQ*. The other drivers were walking around with these big old belt buckles and cowboy hats and they all just looked at Tim and said, 'What in the heck is he doing?'"

Harold Elliott, his old buddy from the Blue Max days, had his own theory.

"The God's truth, I think he was mocking people," Elliott said. "I think that was part of the actor inside of him. He could grow a beard and a mustache in about a week. One day he'd show up looking like he was Hank Williams Jr., wearing a jacket with fringes on it, the next week he'd have on a silk suit. For a while there, people would show up at the track acting like they wanted to look like gangsters. He could do that, too."

In his new ride with Hendrick's team, however, Richmond was no longer representing a beer company. His sponsor, almost ironically, sold coffee—as though the time had come for the party to end and for Richmond to clear his head and start winning races and championships the way he always wanted to do.

But Richmond crashed his car in his 125-mile qualifying race at Daytona, continuing his history of getting his seasons off to a bad start. He lined up 37th at the start of the 500 and didn't wreck this time. But he finished 12 laps down in 20th. What made that even harder to take was that Geoff Bodine won the Daytona 500 with Gary Nelson replacing Harry Hyde as his crew chief. Bodine led 101 of the 200 laps but had Dale Earnhardt on his rear bumper as the race neared its end. Earnhardt, however, dropped off the pace with three laps remaining because he was running out of gas. When he came to pit road for a splash of gas, he cooked his engine as he tried to get back up to speed and finished 14th.

"I thought, dang, I'm smarter than I thought I was," Hendrick said. It was the biggest victory in Hendrick Motorsports history to that point, but Bodine's Daytona 500 triumph also stuck right in the center of Hyde's craw.

Hyde was born in Kentucky. His father, who was a stonecutter, died when he was just nine years old. When Hyde was 15, he lied about his age and joined the Army. He wound up in the South Pacific in World War II with the 38th Infantry and made six amphibious landings before a shrapnel wound got him transferred to the motor pool. After leaving the Army he kept working on cars and wound up in racing.

Bobby Isaac won 36 races in cars that Hyde prepared. Dave Marcis, Buddy Baker, Neil Bonnett and Bodine had also won in his cars.

Hyde was, in a word, irascible. Once while on a plane flying to a race in Phoenix, Hyde and a flight attendant wound up in a disagreement. When the plane hit turbulence and the pilot turned on the sign asking passengers to fasten their seat belts, Hyde did nothing. He merely kept on reading the book on World War II history he'd brought with him. The flight attendant asked Hyde several times to buckle up. Finally, she was fed up. "This is absolutely the last warning I am going to give you," she said to Hyde. "You have to buckle that seat belt."

Hyde finally folded the book, put it on his lap, and for the first time acknowledged that he'd even heard the flight attendant's request. "Darlin'," Hyde said. "Suppose this big bird would nose into the side of that mountain down there. Is it going to make a damn bit of difference when this seat goes flying through the front of it whether my ass is strapped to it or not?"

The conversation was over.

When Tom Higgins heard Hendrick planned to pair Hyde with Richmond, he was amazed.

"I figured there was no damn way it was going to work," Higgins said. "They were totally, totally different. I figured within about two weeks we'd see a mushroom cloud out there over Harrisburg where the shop was."

It took only slightly longer.

In the first 14 races of 1986, Bodine qualified no worse than eighth. He won six poles and started in the first two rows 12 times. In the seven races that he finished, he was in the top 10 seven times. But he crashed out at Richmond International Raceway and had failures in four engines and two camshafts. And he was convinced he knew why.

"Rick gave Harry a lot of control with his teams," Bodine said. "When Tim came along, Harry went with him and I got Gary Nelson, and that was fine. But Gary and I didn't have the pull that Harry had with Rick. Harry had hired all of them; he'd bred them and fed them and all of that. I was leading a lot of laps but I was blowing a lot of engines. It was hard to get good engine parts and cylinder heads. If a team could put together one good engine that was a big thing. Trying to get two good engines for two teams? That was hard. We'd look, and Tim would have the engine that I was supposed to have. A lot of that went on and it hurt our team. We won races, but we would have won a lot more, and maybe the championship. But Harry had the power over everybody, and he used it."

Hendrick, however, was also impressed by Nelson, who would follow his successful career as a crew chief by going to work for NASCAR, for which he now runs its research and development facility in Concord, N.C.

"Gary was pretty innovative and smart," Hendrick said. "He had come up with some stuff on the front ends of the cars and it really worked. He was making his own pieces. One night I took Harry over to show him Gary's cars after everybody had left their shop. I told Gary that I was just going to bring Harry over there. 'You can tell him what you're doing. He won't agree with it, but he'll see it.' We got over there and Harry walked in and starts telling Gary what was wrong with all of his cars. I could see Gary's ears getting red. Harry was saying that all the cars were all messed up, and that Gary needed to do this or that to them. But Harry went back to his shop and starting making some of the same changes to his cars."

That ploy had worked, but it seemed it was going to take an entire team of counselors to get Richmond and Hyde on the same page.

In the first place, Hyde came into the association carrying his own baggage. "I had built this reputation of bringing up young 'uns, and I hated it," Hyde said in an interview quoted in a book issued in 2004 to celebrate the 20th anniversary of the Hendrick team. "It seemed like everybody wanted me to raise their young 'uns, and I wanted an experienced driver. I wanted a David Pearson. I wanted a Richard Petty. I wanted someone who already knew how to drive. Tim was so defiant. He wouldn't stop long enough to listen to anybody. He was his own man and he was going to do it his way—and the car had to do it his way."

Richmond could go fast, there was never any doubting that. In his first 14 races of the 1986 season, Richmond won two poles but qualified in the top three 10 times. Hyde, however, built and set up cars to last. He knew that patience, over the course of a long NASCAR Winston Cup race, could pay off. What he was finding out though, was that his new driver's style ran completely counter to that.

"It took Harry a while to figure out what Tim was talking about," Jimmy Johnson said. "Tim would say, 'The car is looking up the race track,' or, 'Going down the straightaway the car is hunting.' Tim would say 'oversteer' or 'understeer,' and Harry had no clue what that was. They were speaking different languages. We had terrible brake problems. Tim was hard on brakes, and Harry had no clue how to keep brakes under him. One race the brakes got so hot we boiled the fluid and it was spraying on Tim in the car—he was getting burned up, and Harry was telling him to drive harder."

Things bottomed out at Dover, where Richmond blew an engine just 85 laps into the season's 10th race. He finished 32nd among 37 cars. What's worse, Bodine won again.

"Right after that race at Dover, they started into each other one day in this little trailer building I had rented to use as an office there at the shop," Johnson said. "I had to jump up and literally hold them apart, because they were screaming and cussing each other. Tim said, 'You get your ass out of this trailer and I will stomp it!' And out the door Harry went. He was ready. Tim was going out, too, and I was holding him back and then he starts to laugh. Harry said, 'What the hell are you laughing at, you SOB!' Tim said, 'I am just afraid I am going to get my ass beat by a guy who's twice my age.' And Harry started laughing, too."

About that same time, Johnson said, Hyde hired David Oliver to be the team's tire specialist. Oliver understood the alchemy of "stagger," the process of balancing sets of tires based on measuring their circumference. In those days when only biased-ply tires were used in NASCAR, slight differences in the sizes of each tire could be used to affect a car's handling characteristics, and Oliver quickly developed a feel for putting together combinations that helped the No. 25 go faster.

Trying to improve their communication, Hyde and Richmond also went to North Wilkesboro for a very important tire test. Hyde set the car up so it felt the way Richmond wanted it to feel, the way Richmond felt it was fastest and most comfortable. Hyde then had him run 50 laps that way and recorded the lap times. Then Hyde changed the car to the set up he thought it should have. He put on four new tires and told Richmond to drive it the way Hyde wanted him to, backing off earlier going into the corners and not charging every turn on every lap. Trusting Richmond to give him an honest effort, Hyde was confident that if Richmond ran 50 laps that way, the stopwatch would show that the more conservative way would be significantly faster overall.

That's exactly what happened. Richmond could see the lap times, and he could look at the tire wear. As had been the case all the way back when he was in school, showing Richmond something was a lot better than telling him. Now the boy who'd learned to drive by watching his parents do it understood.

That story might seem familiar if you've seen *Days of Thunder.* The scene, like several that would be included in the movie starring Tom Cruise, was true to Hyde's life.

"When Robert Towne came down here to write the screenplay for that movie, he talked to Dale Earnhardt and Richard Petty and everybody," Hendrick said. "But then he talked to Harry. Harry was the master at manipulating people. Harry got him over in that trailer over there and that was the movie. From that point on, the movie was about Harry, and about me and him and about us getting into racing and all of that."

When Richmond blew the engine at Dover and finished 32nd, he fell 385 points behind Earnhardt in the points standings. The date was May 18, but as it turned out, the next day might as well have been January 1, since a whole new season was about to begin.

CHAPTER 12

The first sign that Richmond was about to turn his 1986 season around came on May 25 at Charlotte Motor Speedway. He qualified second for the Coca-Cola 600, but there was nothing new about the No. 25 Chevrolet being fast in qualifying. Bodine had won the pole, giving the Hendrick Motorsports cars a sweep of the front-row positions.

On that Saturday, Richmond drove the team's Robert Gee-prepared No. 15 Pontiac in the Winn-Dixie 300 race in the NASCAR Busch Series. He'd been on the pole for that race, too, and averaged a race-record 139.715 mph to win it for the second straight year. He wore the field out, leading 97 of the last 98 laps.

In the 600 the next day, Bill Elliott was leading late but had to make a late stop for fuel, while Richmond and Earnhardt had the gas to go the distance. Earnhardt wound up winning by 1.59 seconds, with Richmond second. Richmond then finished second again at Riverside after leading 43 laps, losing by a whisker to Darrell Waltrip in a metal-crunching race back to the caution with a lap to go.

The breakthrough came at Pocono on June 8, the day after Richmond's 31st birthday. It had been 64 races since Richmond's last win with Blue Max in 1984, but if that was a drought, then a monsoon was about to set in.

Richmond and Bodine battled for the lead through the first half of the race. On lap 94, Bodine took over the top spot and Earnhardt got around Richmond, too. Two laps later the skies opened. The field completed lap 100 under caution before the red flag was shown, meaning they'd reached the halfway point. But after a delay of nearly two hours, the race resumed under yellow.

Just before 6 p.m., the green came out on lap 119 and Richmond began to take charge. He was out front by more than six seconds with 13 laps to go, but Earnhardt was coming. He'd cut Richmond's lead to less than two seconds with four laps to go, but Buddy Arrington spun in the grass going into Turn 1 and went back up on the track, where he was hit first by Morgan Shepherd and then by Harry Gant. The race ended under caution, and Richmond had scored his fifth career victory and his first for his new team.

"This is a big, big relief," Richmond said. "We've been trying and trying. Sixty-four races is a long time—I hope it isn't as long until the next one."

For Hyde, it was his 40th career victory as a crew chief in 490 races. "Everybody said putting the oldest with the youngest would never work," he said after the celebration in victory lane. "And I'll be honest. I kind of felt the same way. Today, I have nothing but good things to say about him, but next week I might have nothing but bad. He's got so much talent. I've raised a lot of drivers in my time, and Richmond is one of the most aggressive. He'll make you think. He might run 10 laps real fast and 10 laps later he'll be mad as hell because his tires are so heated up that it's not as fast. He'll drive that way from start to finish, just pushing the car. He's got so much determination."

Richmond won the pole for the next race at Michigan, but finished 15th. Next was Daytona, a place Richmond had never seemed to figure out. He had won an Automobile Racing Club of America race there in 1981, and had also won the consolation race after failing to make the Daytona 500 in 1982. But in 10 previous points races there, his average start was 26th and his average finish was 27th. But things were different now.

As soon as the green flag flew to start the Firecracker 400, something either fell off of Morgan Shepherd's car or flew underneath it and came back into Richmond's windshield. Richmond fell well back off the pace as he tried to see where he was going through the cracks and around tape his crew put on the windshield during pit stops.

When rain began to fall, however, the race went under the yellow flag and stayed there for 27 laps until the shower stopped and the track was dry again. During that lull, Richmond was able to come in and have the windshield replaced without losing a lap. While he was there for those repairs, he also got fuel and tires. So when the leaders stopped for fuel on lap 126, Richmond stayed out and picked up ground. Then, when Rodney Combs's Turn 4 spin brought out another yellow on lap 133, Earnhardt, Bobby Allison, Bill Elliott and Cale Yarborough came back to pit road—but did so a lap too early. Sterling Marlin had not yet made his pit stop, and when he went past the drivers sitting on pit road he put them a lap down. Though they got back on the tail end of the lead lap when Marlin made his stop a lap later, those four drivers were now nearly 2.5 miles behind the leaders.

Richmond passed Buddy Baker and took the lead on lap 139, but Baker got it back on lap 146 and seemed to be on his way to victory. But on lap 154, with Baker pulling away, Earnhardt blew an engine going into Turn 1 and went into the wall. Baker dodged Earnhardt's car, but then Connie Saylor spun in front of Baker.

Baker tried to miss Saylor, too, but scraped the Turn 2 wall and knocked his Oldsmobile out of alignment. Richmond, meanwhile, sailed cleanly through everything. He passed Baker and took the lead.

With three laps left, the green came out again and Richmond got a good jump. The leaders had passed Elliott, Allison and Yarborough to put them back down a lap, and on the restart those lapped cars moved into line behind Richmond, giving the leader a buffer from the second-place car driven by Marlin. Richmond won by 1.39 seconds.

"I would definitely say this is my biggest win," said Richmond, who took a victory lap after the checkered flag because he'd always promised himself he'd do that if he ever won at Daytona or Charlotte. "The only trouble was it wasn't the Daytona 500. But I ain't done yet. This track owes me."

In any other life, what happened in the next race would have been impossible to top. The story of the 1986 Summer 500 at Pocono Raceway is one of the most remarkable in NASCAR Winston Cup racing history. It's another of the stories Robert Towne tried to capture in his *Days of Thunder* screenplay, but on film it looks so impossible as to seem farfetched. For all of the people who said that Richmond could do things in a race car that nobody should be able to do, it's the story that backs up that contention.

Richmond was starting fifth in the July 20 race, but on race morning fog, and a heavy mist set in. The scheduled 1:15 p.m. start was delayed until 2:45, and there was no assurance that the bad weather was gone for good.

Early in the race, Richmond was leading but lost ground on a pit stop. Earnhardt had taken the top spot, but before long Richmond had erased that edge and passed him.

"Bodine and Earnhardt were always in a feud with each other," Hendrick said. "When Tim passed Earnhardt, he came over the radio and said, 'Hey Rick, did you like that?' I told him, 'Yeah, that's great.' Then he said, 'Watch this.' He came back around and when he went into Turn 3, I thought he'd blown his engine. He slowed down, pulled up and let Earnhardt go back around him. Earnhardt pulled away a little bit, but when they got to about the flag stand Richmond pulled up behind him and lifted Earnhardt's rear wheels up off the ground with his car. Then he drove on back around him again. Tim was just messing with Earnhardt."

On lap 122, Jim Sauter spun in Turn 1 and the caution came out. With the weather threatening again, it seemed likely that the driver getting back to the line first to take the yellow flag might also win the race.

Richmond, Bodine and Neil Bonnett all wanted to be the leader at the line. But they were three-wide going into Turn 2, the dreaded "Tunnel Turn" at Pocono, where two-wide is ill-advised and three-wide is, well, a wreck. There was contact and Richmond spun into the grass, sending Richard Petty, who had been fourth, crashing into an embankment.

Petty was hot. "I am not going to say who, but some people who call themselves race car drivers caused a needless wreck," he said.

Weeks later, Petty was still stewing.

"Tim doesn't fit the mold of other drivers who have come into this sport and become winners," he said in an interview in NASCAR *Winston Cup Scene*. ". . . If you talk about Allison, Waltrip, Pearson, Cale or myself, those drivers were all aggressive to a certain point. But we all knew our limits. So far, Tim hasn't found a limit. For instance, at Pocono, anybody who has got any kind of limits at all would not have caused what happened."

Richmond had blown out both of his front tires and his left-rear. With the front tires down, the car's frame rails were digging in and the front wheels locked up if Richmond tried to go forward to get his car back to pit road for repairs.

So he turned it around.

"He spun the thing around and drove it backward, halfway around the track, at about 75 mph to beat the pace car so he wouldn't lose another lap," Hendrick said.

He backed it to the entrance to pit road, where the flatter frontstretch allowed him to whirl around again and go, the right way, down pit road. The team changed left-side tires first while the crew did what it could to get the sheet metal straightened out. The pace car was coming around again, though, and the team hadn't changed the right-side tires. No problem. They dropped the jack and Richmond went back out, on three tires with the right-front still flat. He made a lap around the 2.5-mile track and came back to pit road, got right-side tires and restarted the race a lap down.

Richmond clearly had been strong before the wreck, and in a 200-lap race he still had time to make up the ground he'd lost. But the delay at the start of the race and several caution flags during it had made for a long day. Darkness was becoming a factor, so NASCAR informed the teams that the event would be shortened to 150 laps. The green came out again on lap 126, meaning Richmond had 25 laps to make up the one he'd lost and try to salvage the day.

On the first lap after the restart, Morgan Shepherd spun in Turn 2 and four other cars got caught up in the wreck. Richmond pitted again for more work on his car. The green came out again on lap 134 and this time, Richmond got ahead of Waltrip, the leader, to get back on the lead lap. When Earnhardt hit the wall in Turn 2 to bring out a yellow, Richmond came all the way around and lined up sixth, the last car on the lead lap, after coming in for four fresh tires.

With eight laps left it was Bodine, who'd won his fifth pole of the season for the race, in the lead. When Earnhardt hit the Turn 2 wall again after the restart, the yellow came back out. Richmond had made it up to fifth, but when the green flew again there were only four laps remaining. On Lap 148, he passed Waltrip, Bobby Allison and Ricky Rudd.

On the final lap, the Hendrick teammates were side by side, rubbing on each other as they went into the first turn. Richmond nosed in front coming off that turn, but by the exit of Turn 2, Bodine was ahead. On the short chute between Turn 2 and Turn 3, Richmond stayed on the outside with the new tires Hyde had given him on the last pit stop helping him gain grip in the high line. He and Bodine banged fenders several times as they came off the sharp third turn and made like drag racers as they headed for the checkered flag.

But here came Rudd. As the Hendrick cars jostled each other, Rudd rallied in his Bud Moore-owned Ford and suddenly had a run on the inside. In the final 100 yards of what wound up being a 375-mile race, he gobbled up ground.

When the cars slashed across the finish line, Richmond knew he'd held off Bodine. But he didn't know if he'd beaten Rudd's late charge.

"We got down to the first turn after the checkered flag and Ricky and I pulled alongside each other," Richmond said. "He pointed at me as if to say, 'Did you win?' I shrugged and pointed to him. He laughed and shrugged. Neither of us really knew."

Neither did NASCAR, at least not without checking the photo from a camera it had stationed at the line for just such a finish. Rudd and Richmond both pulled their cars to the entrance of victory lane as the 65,000 fans, wrung out from a long day and from the incredible finish, cheered. Several minutes passed before officials waved Richmond into victory lane. He'd won by less than a foot— the official margin of victory was set at 0.05 seconds. Bodine was less than a car-length behind, but he finished third.

Richmond was rolling. When he finished second in the next race at Talladega, behind only 22-year-old phenom Bobby Hillin Jr., Richmond had won three times and finished second in three more races in his past seven starts. Since the season's third race, he'd qualified outside the top 10 only once and outside the top five only three times in 15 races. In that seven-race span he'd moved up to third in the points race, and now trailed Earnhardt by just 185 points. Waltrip was only 24 points ahead of him in second.

"Everybody else knew that we just had to ride it out," Kyle Petty said of Richmond's streak. "They were feeling like they could do no wrong, like they could push the car off the back of the trailer and not even put down the lift gate. They could let the car hit the ground and still go out and sit on the pole. That's how you feel as a team when it's going like that, and as competitors all you could do was let it run its course. Sometimes, you knew that all you could do was run for second."

Barry Dodson was still at Blue Max Racing. The team had hired Rusty Wallace to replace Richmond, and Wallace won at Bristol in the season's fifth race, earning his first career NASCAR Cup victory.

"We won before Tim did in 1986," Dodson said. "He was the first one, and the only one, to stop his car on pit road where our crew was and say congratulations. But when we won first, I think all we did was tick him off."

The only thing hotter than Richmond that summer was the weather in the Southeast. It had been dry, too, so dry cities in the Carolinas, Georgia and Alabama were placing restrictions on water use. As they drove to Talladega for the race Eddie Thrap and Johnny Hayes, two veterans of the NASCAR garage, noticed how brown everything looked in the fields along the highways. They'd heard that grain would need to be shipped from the Midwest, which had received ample rain, to the Southeast, and since there was no Cup race the following weekend they felt some of the teams in NASCAR could lend a hand.

The project began as talk among a few people in the garage. Within days, it had mushroomed into something much larger. By the end of the following week, nearly 100 businesses had pledged support and 43 trucks were secured to travel to Ohio, pick up 30,000 bales of hay and bring it back to the Southeast.

On Friday, August 1, the trucks gathered at Charlotte Motor Speedway for what by then was billed as the "Hayride 500." Dozens of NASCAR teams loaned the tractors used to pull their transporters to the tracks to the effort, with their transporter drivers at the wheel. But the No. 25 Hendrick Motorsports team's truck had a different kind of driver in it. Richmond cleared his schedule and spent the off weekend making the trip up and back to Ohio, lending star quality that brought more publicity and support to the effort.

It was the summer of 1986, and the top movie in theaters across America was about a hotshot young fighter pilot earning his wings. It starred a young actor who was rapidly becoming one of Hollywood's biggest attractions, Tom Cruise, who one day would be cast in the lead role in a movie about stock-car racing playing a character with the same kind of cocksure attitude his fighter pilot's character had in that year's big hit.

So as the Hayride 500 headed out of Charlotte, the drivers stayed in contact over citizen band radios. Most of them drove every weekend, so they already had a "handle," a name they used on the CB. Richmond, however, needed one, and the name of the Tom Cruise movie seemed like a good fit. So they called him "Top Gun."

C H A P T E R   13

Richmond came to upstate New York in August of 1986 with the NASCAR world on a string.

"If you had your choice of spending a day with any driver who'd ever raced in NASCAR, you'd spend it with him," Rick Hendrick said. "He had no arrogance about being a driver. He'd walk into a restaurant and climb up on the table and introduce himself. He didn't need bodyguards. He'd go out in the parking lot and sign autographs for the fans. He just loved life and he'd wade right into it. If there was a good-looking girl within 100 yards, he'd have his arm around her.

"He was a rock star. There were 40-year-old women who'd wet their britches to meet him, and their husbands would be standing right there with a Tim Richmond t-shirt on."

The sponsors, Hendrick said, were tickled by Richmond's surge of success and also by the way he was working with them.

"Tim was changing," Hendrick said. "All of the reputation came from before he was with us. He was still having a good time, but it was nothing like the stuff we'd heard before. He made his appearances, he made the photo shoots, he was doing everything he was supposed to do. He was a model guy."

People on both sides of the garage fence were noticing Richmond and Hyde and the success they were having. Bodine believed that Hyde was taking all of the best engines built by Randy Dorton's motor department at Hendrick Motorsports. Some of the other teams in the garage were trying to figure out what else the No. 25 team might be up to, and in that regard it was Hyde's reputation, not Richmond's, that had them suspicious.

"Every week in NASCAR you've got a race winner and 40-some other guys who got cheated," Chip Williams said. "We always heard that kind of stuff. We'd heard it when Bill Elliott won 11 races in 1985. People would come to us and say, 'Here's what they're doing, you need to check this out.' And it would be something different every time.

"Harry considered himself lucky because he was getting to do something he absolutely loved to do. He had so much fun racing when he was winning. He'd come in one time and been sort of pushed out, and now Tim was letting him come back. The whole thing was a game he got paid for playing. Harry would spend more time trying to figure out a way to get around a rule, legally or illegally, than he would trying to get his car ready to race. He loved doing that, and he'd raced with or knew just about every driver who was in the garage."

Two men who'd started the year at each other's throats were now getting along famously. Hyde would accompany Richmond to sponsor appearances and they'd trade barbs like a Vaudeville comedy team, with Tim dressed in a white leisure suit and a pink shirt standing beside Hyde in his blue jeans and Folgers team baseball cap.

"Harry realized what he had in Tim," Hendrick said. "And Tim realized what he had, too, a crew chief and somebody he could look up to like he did his father. Harry had worked all of his life and realized he had something now like nothing he'd ever had before."

Hyde certainly knew Richmond was different in many ways.

"Tim has the ability to burn the wheels off a car," he said in a story in *NASCAR Winston Cup Scene* that August. "Even if a car is not handling well, he'll drive it just as hard as he can. I've never seen him back off and don't want him to back off the last part of the race. But sometimes he wants to race too much too quick. He doesn't want to bide his time.

"He gets to the track when he's supposed to get here. But it might take him 30 minutes or an hour to get from the parking lot to the race car. He does interviews, he signs autographs, or he talks to fans, you know. And I'm standing here waiting to talk to him about the race car. . . . When he gets in that race car he is one of the most dedicated drivers I've ever seen. He's serious as hell. But when he hits the ground he's hot-damned Hollywood plus."

Hyde and "Hollywood," along with the rest of the circuit, headed to upstate New York to visit the historic road course at Watkins Glen, N.Y., in mid-August of 1986. Tom Higgins went up early to write a story about The Glen, which from 1961 until 1980 was the site for Formula One's Grand Prix racing in the United States. Higgins had a longtime friend who grew up in the area and had worked at the track during the F1 years.

"He took me around to all of these great old places," Higgins said. "We went around the old course that was there when they really ran through the country. Finally, we wound up at the Seneca Lodge. It had an aura that was almost spooky. You'd go in the place and it was dark, it had this dark wood everywhere. Wreaths were hanging on the wall that they'd put around the necks of the drivers who won the Formula 1 race. It was spooky, these things were brittle and dried out, all brown. It gave you cold chills. I wrote a story about that and how the winner always went there after the race.

The winning driver would stand on the bar and the crew would throw beer on him."

Richmond won the pole for the Budweiser at The Glen and found himself locked in a battle with Darrell Waltrip for the victory as the 90-lap race wound down. As much as Richmond and Earnhardt enjoyed messing with each other, there wasn't a lot of love lost between Richmond and Waltrip.

"Tim was running late getting to the track one day at Charlotte," Tim Brewer said. "Darrell came over and asked me if I needed anything. I said, 'Yeah, I could use a plug check.' So DW went out and got us a plug check. He came back in after driving our car and said, 'Just what I thought, Brewer. You've got a pretty good car, there's just something wrong with the interior.'"

Hendrick, however, was still growing his racing empire. In late June, he announced that he'd signed a deal to bring Waltrip to start yet a third team, this one sponsored by another Procter & Gamble brand—Tide detergent—with engine builder extraordinaire Waddell Wilson coming along to form what the NASCAR community was already calling a "super team."

In the summer of 1986, though, the super team was Richmond's. On lap 79, he slipped past Waltrip in Turn 5 at the end of the track's long backstretch to grab the lead and held on the rest of the way.

Two months earlier, Richmond had four career NASCAR Cup victories. In six races, he'd doubled that total. With four wins and three seconds, the $50,955 he won at Watkins Glen gave him winnings of $334,480 in his past eight races—nearly as much as the $345,848 it took him 30 races to win the year before.

He also put his name on the list of winners at Watkins Glen, but Hyde had something a little more permanent in mind. Hyde had heard about the traditional winner's celebration at the Seneca Lodge, so after the postrace festivities the team went there.

"Guys who win NASCAR races don't get wreaths put around their necks because that would cover up the sponsors' logos on the uniforms," Higgins said. "Tim got really upset because they had nothing to put up on the wall. "Harry said, 'Heck, we'll hang a tire up there.' He sent David Oliver out to crawl under the car in the truck that was parked outside and he get a tire. They hung it on the wall, and I imagine it's still hanging up there."

At Michigan, Richmond was caught on pit road when a caution came out, trapping him a lap down. But with less than 20 laps left, he made the lap up and came storming back from 14th to second behind Bill Elliott, who scored his fourth straight NASCAR Cup victory at that track. Richmond won the pole for the night race at Bristol, but never quite got the handling right and finished two laps down in sixth as Waltrip got the victory.

It had been two whole races since Richmond had won, so when he got to Darlington for the Southern 500 he was ready to go. He and Bodine once again swept the front-row spots in qualifying, with Richmond winning another pole. Just 14 laps into the race, rain began to fall and the field waited two hours, 15 minutes to get back on the track. Richmond and Bodine dominated the race, leading 348 laps between them, and Bodine was in front with Earnhardt between him and Richmond on lap 320 when Earnhardt blistered a tire and had to make a pit stop, losing a lap.

When a yellow came out on lap 331, the rest of the leaders made fuel stops, but Bodine elected to stay on the track. Gary Nelson never expected Bodine's car to make it to the end of the scheduled 500 miles without more fuel, he was gambling that the rain that had caused the caution would keep falling and end the race early with Bodine out front.

The rain, however, ceased, and the racing resumed. On lap 354, Bodine was out of fuel and on his way to pit road. Bill Elliott, who'd taken just two tires and come off pit road first, inherited the lead and was more than a second ahead of Richmond. But on lap 361 Elliott got into the wall in Turns 1 and 2 and nearly spun out. Richmond seized the opportunity and, on the next lap, reclaimed the lead and went on to win.

"I think I would rather win a race on it than any other track," Richmond said. "Now I've won the Southern 500. If I ever get any grandchildren—heck, if I ever have any children—I'll be able to show them the pictures. When you win at Darlington you have beaten the odds."

The victory was gratifying for Hyde, too, who'd never had one of his cars win at Darlington. Hyde laughed when he came to the press box in Turn 1 of the historic track, where the Southern 500 had been run on Labor Day weekend since 1950, because he'd had a hand in getting it built to replace the old open press box. In 1967, Earl Balmer's car had crashed and got up on the guard rail, sawing the car almost in half and spraying gas on the reporters.

The remarkable run that Richmond, Hyde and their team had put together was still not over. At Richmond International Raceway, the No. 25 fell a lap down in the middle of the Wrangler Indigo 500 when an overheating axle put too much heat on its rear tires. But the team kept working on the problem, and when Ken Schrader wrecked on lap 310 to bring out a yellow flag, Richmond got back on the lead lap.

Tommy Ellis wrecked on lap 340 and dumped a lot of fluid on the track. NASCAR put down a large amount of a dust used to dry up that fluid, and when the race restarted, Rusty Wallace and Rudd both got loose in it and hit the wall. Richmond had no such problem and drove into the lead. He kept it the rest of the way.

It had been a remarkable 12-race stretch.

Since the runner-up finish at Charlotte in May, Richmond had won six times and finished second four times. He'd won three poles and never started worse than ninth. He'd led at least five laps in every race and a total of 601 laps in that span. He won more than

$450,000. And he'd climbed past Waltrip into second in the NASCAR Winston Cup standings, just 118 points behind Earnhardt.

Richmond had been waiting his entire career for the roll he'd been on through the summer of 1986.

"I've been hearing for what seems like forever that I was going to be the next superstar," Richmond said after one of his wins. "I'm ready for that day to arrive."

He joked about seeing a magazine ad featuring Baltimore Orioles pitcher Jim Palmer wearing nothing but underwear.

"I might even get a Jockey advertisement," he joked. "I can't wait to start taking my clothes off. . . . A couple of years ago I took some acting lessons and wanted to be a movie star for all the wrong reasons—money, women and fame. Well, maybe those weren't exactly the wrong reasons, but I am more serious about it now."

But by mid-September, the people around Tim Richmond began to notice that he seemed to be feeling less than 100 percent. At Darlington, before the Southern 500 victory, Hyde said it seemed like Richmond had a cold or perhaps the touch of the flu.

"Tim just kept getting sick like that for several weeks late that season," Sandy Welsh said. "He'd go to a doctor and they'd put him on antibiotics and he'd get better. He'd go off the antibiotics and he'd start feeling sick again."

On the track, the breaks began to even out a little bit and Richmond's surge slowed dramatically. He finished only 299 laps in a 500-lap race at Dover and wound up 26th, his worst finish since the Dover race earlier that year. He was 10th at Martinsville and 11th at North Wilkesboro, and fell back to third behind Waltrip in the standings. Still, coming to Charlotte in October, he was only 144 points back. With another streak, he might still make things uncomfortable for his old pal Dale Earnhardt.

"They used to do four-lap qualifying runs at Charlotte, and Tim would put an extra 5,000 fans in the seats just to watch him,"

Hendrick said. "He would come off Turn 4 and graze the wall every time in exactly the same place. From just behind the rear tire to the back bumper of the car, he would skim it, just enough to knock the paint off. And he would do it every single lap. That's all car control—that, and cojones as big as watermelons."

Richmond's top lap speed in his four-lap run that week was 169.252 mph. His four-lap average of 167.078 mph was good enough for his second straight pole, his sixth of the season. When the Oakwood Homes 500 began, Richmond took off. At one point, Earnhardt was two laps down but he made those up, and by the midway point in the race he and Richmond put on a show. Between them, they led 134 of 135 laps over one stretch, and during it they spent nearly three laps racing door to door. Finally Earnhardt got too high in Turn 2 and scraped along the wall, allowing Richmond to pull away and convincing Earnhardt, the points leader, that play time with Richmond was over.

"I was having so much fun," Earnhardt said. "I just got caught up in the competition and the fun we were having and forgot there was still a lot of racing to do. When I hit the wall, it sort of calmed me down."

In all, Richmond led 123 laps that day. But after 266 laps, his engine failed. Richmond finished 27th and Earnhardt won the race. Richmond now trailed by 232 points with three races left, and his shot at a championship was done. He won another pole at Rockingham but finished 20th, and then was fourth at Atlanta as Earnhardt clinched the title with another win.

Richmond, meanwhile, kept fighting whatever the ailment was that had been bothering him for weeks.

"He went to this clinic in Texas and went through I don't know how many days of tests down there," Welsh said. "They couldn't find anything. He was always sick, but nobody could tell him why."

Hyde was worried. By Rockingham, Richmond didn't look well at all. Still, in the season's final race at Riverside, he won his eighth pole of the season, tying Bodine for the most that season. He then passed Earnhardt for the lead on Lap 109 of 119 and went on to score his seventh victory, more than anyone all year, and missed catching Waltrip for second in the standings by just six points.

"I remember Richard Childress coming over to me," Hendrick said, referring to the owner of Earnhardt's championship-winning car. "He said that the way we were running he knew if they wanted to win another championship in 1987 they'd have to beat us. That was big, it was like God coming over and saying he was impressed with us."

Richmond had made plans to spend time between the end of the 1986 season and the start of the 1987 season in Southern California, trying to get his career as an actor off the ground. Instead, after the Riverside race he went to a doctor that someone had recommended to him and had more tests done.

He also took his mother, Evelyn, shopping on Rodeo Drive in Beverly Hills. He'd already purchased a dress for Sandy Welsh to wear to the NASCAR Winston Cup Awards Ceremony in New York, where the top 10 in the standings are honored after every year.

"Tim was in Florida one year before Christmas and he called," Welsh said. "He was Christmas shopping with Julie Beckwith, a woman that he cared about a lot, and he wanted to know what kind of dress to buy me. He took Mother to Rodeo Drive and bought her a dress and shoes and earrings. And of course he'd picked out his tuxedo for the banquet, too."

The banquet was held on Friday, December 5 in the Grand Ballroom of the Waldorf-Astoria Hotel in midtown Manhattan, and although Richmond was decked out in sartorial splendor, it was obvious to just about everyone who saw him that he was not well.

"Drivers who finished second through 10th in the standings stood in the wings off stage as they waited to go on stage," Chip

Williams said. "I was kind of like the floor director that night. Tim had on a tuxedo with a white tie on, and he just looked pale. He was sweating, too, but I figured that was nerves. The other guys back there were nervous and sweating, too. But he went up on stage and did his deal, but when I looked back on it later you could tell he just wasn't feeling very well."

On Monday, December 8, Richmond flew to Chicago where he was to do publicity for a midget race he'd agreed to run in. When the plane landed, Richmond would say later, he felt so bad he didn't think he could walk 10 feet.

Somehow, he made it to his hotel and did some of the press interviews he had scheduled via telephone. He also took a call from his doctor in California.

The mystery behind his illness was over.

He had AIDS.

CHAPTER 14

That night, Richmond called Sandy Welsh.

"He was so, so sick," said Welsh, who was in Ashland. "I stayed on the phone talking to him most of the night. The next day, he got his doctor to call me the next day and explain to me what he had."

The specific diagnosis was pneumocystis pneumonia, an opportunistic strain of pneumonia spread via a common parasite that people with healthy immune systems are able to fight off easily. But in victims with weakened immune systems, the parasite can create a severe, life-threatening infection of the lungs. Its presence in Richmond's body indicated an even more frightening condition.

In the still brief clinical history of the disease, the strain of pneumonia had emerged as a marker in patients likely infected with HIV, the virus that causes acquired immune deficiency syndrome—AIDS.

"He didn't want Mom and Al to know," Welsh said. "He made me promise not to tell them. Somehow the next day, he left the hotel, got on an airplane and got himself to Charlotte."

Evelyn Richmond picked Tim up and took him to his house on Lake Norman.

"I was in Ashland and I had to do the company payroll that morning," Welsh said. "I told Al that as soon as I got that done we needed to get to North Carolina. I told him I couldn't tell him why but we had to get there."

Al obviously knew something was seriously wrong. "He thought Tim had tuberculosis," Welsh said. "I said, 'No, that's not it. But we have to get down there.' We got on a plane, flew to Charlotte and rented a car. It was pouring rain, a miserable night, and drove up to the house. Mom was upset that we were even there. She thought Tim just needed to rest. She was angry. The motor home was there, and Al went out and got in it to go to bed. Mom and I were sitting there in the living room.

"She said, 'You know what's wrong with Tim, don't you?' I told her I did. I said, 'Mom, how would you react if Tim had AIDS?' She wasn't really sure what it was, either, but as I explained it to her she just went to pieces. She ran out to the motor home and told Al. He came in and they went back to see Tim. Tim was angry at me for telling them, but I told him that they had to know."

The next morning, Welsh got on the phone with the doctors in California.

"They said, 'You have got to get him to a hospital,' and they gave us choices of where to go. One of the places was the Cleveland Clinic, and Tim said he'd go there because the folks still owned a house in Ohio and it was closer. The doctor in California called the clinic and made the arrangements to get him in there under an assumed name."

Welsh and Richmond flew to Cleveland immediately. A car had been arranged to take them to the clinic, but red-tape delays kept cropping up as Welsh tried to get Richmond admitted. A call to the doctor in California help cut through that, and Richmond checked in under the name Lee Warner—his middle name and Evelyn's maiden name.

Al and Evelyn closed up Richmond's house in North Carolina and left in the motor home to drive to Ohio.

"We weren't even sure Tim would make it until they got there," Welsh said. "I sat up in the chair all night with him. He couldn't believe this was happening to him. He said, 'Well if it has to be, the one good thing is I am going to die before Mom and Dad do. I couldn't deal with that.' I said, 'You are not going to die and leave me with them.' That was kind of a joke with us."

Richmond's lungs had filled with fluid and, over the course of a three-week stay in the clinic he lost nearly 25 pounds. In the early years of AIDS treatment, up to 85 percent of patients contracted pneumocystis pneumonia, and until drugs were found that could effectively combat it, that was among the leading primary causes of death of patients with the disease. But Richmond's condition gradually improved. Finally, just after New Year's Day, he was well enough to leave the hospital and go to Ashland.

Evelyn had called Rick Hendrick and told Tim's team owner what was going on. Hendrick got on his plane and flew to Ohio. "Rick Hendrick is a very nice man," Welsh said. "He didn't understand AIDS any better than we did. Mom called him when we found out what Tim had. He got in his plane and landed at the airport in Mansfield. We went and got him and brought him to the house in Ashland. It was pouring down rain again that day, too. Tim was laying on the couch and we were trying to explain what this disease was."

In 1986, AIDS was a disease about which there almost was more misguided misinformation than scientific knowledge. Today, it is widely believed that the virus that causes it came into the human population from a species of chimpanzees, perhaps through contact with blood during hunting and field dressing of the animals. The virus was first known in America, Africa and Haiti as early as 1977. Rare types of pneumonia, cancer and other ailments were reported to doctors in New York and California in 1979.

The disease that would come to be known as AIDS was first mentioned in the American media in May of 1981 when the *New York Native*, a newspaper covering that city's gay community, carried a report of a strange new ailment being seen among homosexual men. A few weeks later, two doctors in Los Angeles reported on five patients suffering from mysterious ailments in a weekly report issued by the Centers for Disease Control. The disease came to be known by several names, including gay-related immune deficiency (GRID) or, colloquially, "the gay plague," before in 1982 the CDC officially established the name acquired immune deficiency syndrome. In 1984, the virus responsible for weakening the immune system was identified as human immunodeficiency virus, or HIV. The virus essentially attacks white blood cells that play an essential role in the body's immune system.

According to today's research, the average time between infection and the appearance of signs that could lead to an AIDS diagnosis is around seven years. Though that time varies, it's possible that Richmond had AIDS before he ever drove a stock car.

The first nationally known person to publicly admit he had AIDS was actor Rock Hudson, a handsome leading man who'd starred in films with Doris Day and in television's *McMillan and Wife* with Susan Saint James. Hudson, who had a role in the 1980s television show *Dynasty* near the end of his life, died on October 2, 1985.

By early 1987, the "mainstream" world still was not dealing with AIDS very well. "Back in those days, it was a black mark," Hendrick said. "It wasn't like it is today when people can stand up and try to make a difference. Back then, it was the equivalent of leprosy."

The best research at the time indicated that HIV was spread through the exchange of bodily fluids. People who had unprotected sexual activity, blood transfusions or who shared needles in intravenous drug use were identified as high-risk groups. But while there was no medically supported evidence that HIV could be spread by casual contact, the disease was seen as a death sentence and few were willing to take a chance such evidence might be found. In 1987, officials at one domestic airline in the United States were forced to end a non-publicized company policy to deny reservations to patients known to have AIDS when reports that the policy existed were confirmed. In Toronto, a panel discussion aired as public affairs television programming centered on whether AIDS patients should be quarantined from the rest of society.

There was an additional component in the stigma of AIDS, too. The disease had first presented itself in the culture of the gay community in major cities, where "bathhouses" provided rendezvous points for casual, promiscuous sexual activity. Homophobia still exists today in American culture, but in 1987 it was far more prevalent. Bigotry and intolerance had no problem taking root, and professional sports—especially one with its foundations in the South—were particularly fertile ground.

"We were still a backwater, Southeastern sport," Kyle Petty said. "AIDS happened in big cities, among gay people or drug abusers. The idea of having that infiltrate the infield at Talladega or Darlington or come to North Wilkesboro scared people. We didn't understand it, and when you're not educated about something, you get right back to the Salem witch hunts."

As Richmond sat in his parents' house in Ashland in early January, slowly trying to get his strength back, it quickly became obvious that he would not be able to drive the No. 25 Chevrolet when the NASCAR season began. He also knew that people would ask why, and he considered the reaction if he told everyone the entire truth.

"People think he tried to keep it hush hush because he had something to hide," Welsh said. "But he didn't want to put his mother and father through what you read about AIDS and the stigma that was attached to it. They were prominent people in Ashland, business owners. Mother had the condo in Florida that she'd owned since Tim was in school down there. Tim loved it down there, and he figured they'd be thrown out of there—or stoned to death or whatever. That was his concern."

To be certain, Richmond was protective of his parents, especially of Evelyn, who had always been right by her son's side. From the time Evelyn Richmond watched on television as her only son wrecked horribly in an Indy car at Michigan, she went to the track with him.

"Mother started going to the races, and at first she would sit in the motor home and cry for fear that something was going to happen to Tim," Welsh said. "But she wanted to be there in case an accident happened again. She finally got to where she could watch. She knew she wasn't going to be able to stop Tim from racing, but she felt stock cars were a little safer, and so she felt like she was somewhat controlling the environment.

"You didn't butt heads with Mother. She was going to be there and nobody was going to stop her. She was a wonderful cook, and people in the garage would come over to the motor home and she'd make them their favorites."

Barry Dodson said Evelyn was a worrier. "She was a good woman, and she absolutely loved Tim to death," he said. "She was protective, as any mom is, I guess. But she never caused problems like some wives or girlfriends do when they're at the track."

Fred Miller said he compares Al Richmond's role in Tim's life to the role played by John Bickford, stepfather to current NASCAR star Jeff Gordon. Like Bickford did for Gordon, Al helped his son make the right career choices to reach the level he had by the end of 1986. "He came off like this real gruff guy, but he was the greatest," Miller said.

As for Evelyn?

"Tim was her boy," Miller said. "In her eyes, Tim could do no wrong. If you told Evelyn that Tim smoked a joint, she wouldn't believe it. It was a little bit overboard, to say the least. It drove Al crazy, but he let it slide because he went and did his own thing."

Tim Brewer said there were times when he tried to enlist Evelyn as an ally in his bid to get Richmond to get to the track on time or focus more on the race car. "We'd get on her occasionally, asking her to get on our side once in a while," Brewer said. "One time I told her, 'He ain't Jesus, he makes mistakes like everybody else.'"

As much as he cared about his parents' reputation, though, Richmond's own desire to be loved and accepted also had to be part of his thought process as he began to deal with the hand he'd been dealt. Everyone who knew much at all about Richmond will tell you that he feared nothing worse than being booed. He once told an interviewer that he could hear boos in a crowd of 50,000 even if almost everyone was cheering. Time after time throughout his career, he kept telling the story about the fan he saw as he took his cool-down lap following his first career victory at Riverside, the man who gave Richmond the finger as he went by and, in Richmond's words, "took the polish" off the win.

And so, a circle began to close. Richmond convinced himself that by staying quiet about his prognosis he was protecting his family—especially Evelyn. Meanwhile, Evelyn was not about to allow anything that she thought might hurt the son she loved so much, and no one else in the family dared to cross her.

There also was the rationalization that saying Richmond was recovering from a serious bout with pneumonia was not a lie. It wasn't AIDS that put him in the hospital in December and still left

him so weak in January that he wasn't yet able to travel from Ohio
where it was winter to the condominium in south Florida, where
he could have recovered while sitting on the 16th floor watching
sailboats on the ocean out the window. It was pneumocystis pneumonia.

Tom Higgins was at the Christmas party that Richmond's team
shared with Bodine's at Hendrick Motorsports down in Charlotte,
and when he asked about Richmond's absence he was told the
driver was in Ohio recovering from a bout with pneumonia.

On January 7, as he returned to work after a holiday break,
Higgins decided to check on Richmond's health. He found
Richmond in Ashland and, for the first time, learned just how bad
the pneumonia had been. "Another day or so," Richmond told
Higgins, "and the doctors say I might . . . well . . . might not have
made it."

Richmond also told Higgins that it looked like he was going to
have to miss the first part of the 1987 season. "As much as I hate to
do it," he said, "that's what my doctor recommends. And I've got
to be realistic about it."

The National Motorsports Press Association, a group of media
that covers racing, holds its annual convention each January. In
1986, it was held in Charlotte in the same week as Charlotte Motor
Speedway conducted its annual preseason "media tour" that allows
writers to visit teams' shops and get interviews for their stories
leading up to the Daytona 500. Richmond was to be honored along
with Dale Earnhardt as co-winners of the NMPA's driver of the
year award, but he was unable to attend. He participated via tele-
conference instead, fielding questions about his condition and
vowing to be back in the car as soon as he was able.

The rumor mill, meanwhile, was cranking up.

"The first thing everybody thought of, I guess, was some kind
of cancer," Chip Williams said. "As it went on into the season a lit-

tle bit, you started hearing things about his lungs and, possibly, tuberculosis."

Somehow, the tuberculosis rumor morphed into a story that Richmond had damaged his lungs while freebasing cocaine. The drug rumors that had dogged Richmond since back in his days in Indy cars certainly were given new life by the speculation of what was really wrong with Richmond.

"Nobody really knew and, from NASCAR's standpoint, we really weren't in a position to ask," Williams said. "[We] would call every once in a while and ask Tim how he was feeling, but he hadn't tried to come back so there really wasn't any way to ask, 'What's wrong?' or anything like that.'"

"Back at that time," Higgins said, "you have to remember that anytime anybody famous got sick, any kind of movie star or sports star, immediately you heard whispers that it was something really, really bad."

Rumors of AIDS were in the wind, too.

"Earnhardt told me that Tim had AIDS," Barry Dodson said. "I knew that was bull, there was no way. The only thing anybody had ever heard about AIDS was Rock Hudson, and the whole world knew Rock Hudson was gay. I knew Tim Richmond wasn't gay."

Richmond eventually got strong enough to go to Florida to stay in the condo in the Fort Lauderdale area. Doctors at The Cleveland Clinic referred him to Dr. David Dodson, who still practices in West Palm Beach.

"I wasn't a diehard NASCAR fan, so I really didn't know Tim before that," Dr. Dodson said. "He was just a great guy. He would come into our office and people would come up and talk to him. He was just as nice as he could have possibly been to everybody around."

Dr. Dodson said he doesn't recall Richmond every asking "Why me?" in regard to his diagnosis.

"We had a conversation about AIDS and death, and he said he wasn't afraid of dying," Dr. Dodson said. "He said that when you're racing and your car is inches away from another going 200 mph, you have to know that anything can happen.

"Early on in the AIDS epidemic, the treatments were just not very good. It was a scary disease. Part of it with Tim was he wanted to be clear that he didn't get it through drug use. He hated needles. There are only certain ways you get AIDS, and I am sure Tim had a lady in every city. I am sure that it was sexually acquired."

Not even his closest friends and staunchest supporters claim that Richmond was sexually monogamous. "Tim was bad about going out with strippers and club girls around Miami," Raymond Beadle said. "He didn't cull real well."

Richmond also at times employed prostitutes, and the possibility that some of them might have been exposed to intravenous drug users or bisexual male partners and were, without their knowledge, carrying HIV in their bodies broadens further the risk factors Richmond could have come in contact with.

"Tim liked having a good time," Fred Miller said. "He'd bring three or four girls home, and it was one for everybody. There's no telling where he got AIDS from, but none of us should be alive if he was going to die from that."

CHAPTER 15

Rick Hendrick hired Benny Parsons, a former NASCAR Winston Cup champion who'd go on to a successful career as a NASCAR television analyst after his retirement, to drive until Richmond could return in 1987. Parsons' car would carry the Folgers sponsorship and the number 35 instead of Richmond's 25.

The 1973 champion had run 16 races in 1986 for the team owned by Richard and Leo Jackson, having run a full season most recently in 1981 for Bud Moore. Parsons had won only one race since 1981, a victory at Atlanta in 1984.

Parsons started well, finishing second to Bill Elliott in the Daytona 500 and second again, three races later, at Atlanta.

Richmond, meanwhile, was finally beginning to get back on his feet. He spent about six weeks in Florida, and his first foray into physical activity was bowling in early March. He was so tired he was ready to quit after one game. He tried to play a little golf and a little tennis, too, quitting for a few days when he got tired then starting back up again. He also talked his way out of a couple of speeding tickets on Interstate 95 in Florida.

In late March, he flew from Miami to Charlotte and went to his house on the lake for the first time since leaving to go to the hospital in Cleveland in December.

Charlotte Observer columnist Tom Sorensen, to whom Richmond had taken a liking in several interviews they'd done over the years, talked to the driver on the phone the day he got back to North Carolina and asked him about the swirling rumors.

"It's actually been kind of flattering," Richmond said in denying that he had AIDS. "I was more or less surprised, amazed and flattered that I got that kind of attention. Not that I liked it, but it's human nature, I guess. But I would feel it was more human nature to say it about Burt Reynolds or Mick Jagger or Bruce Springsteen. I'm flattered if I'm in that category."

Richmond also denied that the problem was cocaine. "I've heard that ever since I showed up here," he said. "It's not true. I guess that's not surprising, either. I'm one of the only single guys down here, and my hair is not the shortest. I've never seen it down here, ever. Fans have come up and offered it, and I said no thanks. It used to be status to have a tennis court or a pool or a boat. Now it's status to be in the Betty Ford Center. But I am thankful to say I wasn't."

Sorensen got a sense that Richmond was choosing his words carefully.

"Let me put it this way," Richmond said. "It's people's nature to know something bigger and better than the next person the first time they open their mouth. And one of the biggest places I've noticed that is in racing."

Richmond told Sorensen that he'd already passed one test. When he arrived in Charlotte, Richmond overheard two airline employees talking. "Wow," one said, nudging the other. "Look there, it's Tim Richmond." Richmond admitted that made him smile.

But he was concerned, too. The next day, March 31, Richmond was going to Darlington to drive a race car for the first time since his victory at Riverside in the final race of the 1986 season. He estimated that he was 60 percent back to where he'd been before he got sick but said he was eager to at least try to see how he could do in the car. "I hope I can make at least one lap," he said.

The test was supposed to be a secret. But word was out and reporters showed up.

"It was cold and Tim was really fast," Jimmy Johnson said. "Steve Waid (from *NASCAR Winston Cup Scene*) and Tom Higgins found out about it, and when we got there, there was a TV camera crew in the infield. Harry went up to them, and the cameraman was this big guy. Harry told them they had to leave, but they said the speedway had let them in.

"Harry said, 'I don't care, I am paying the rental and you have to leave.' They acted like they were leaving but didn't, and Harry saw them around the corner. Harry walked around and grabbed the cameraman by the arm and said, 'I will stick that camera up your ass and stick you in that trash can if you don't leave right now.' I had tears rolling down my face I was laughing so hard.

"They left, but Higgins and Waid were in the press box and we knew they were there. It was getting late and Harry said, 'I am going to show them something.'"

What the reporters didn't know was that Hyde, borrowing a trick that Tim Brewer had once drawn a five-lap penalty for at Martinsville, put two left-side tires on the right side of the car to give Richmond more grip. Richmond shot around the 1.366-mile track in 30.71 seconds—160.600 mph. He then clicked off a lap at 160.340 mph and another at 159.920 mph before rolling off the track and to the truck to be loaded after running a total of 38 laps. The official track record, set by Bodine in winning the pole for the 1986 spring race at Darlington, was 159.197 mph. All three of Richmond's laps on the final run were faster.

Hyde was practically giddy.

"They say I am a tough old man," he said. "And I guess I do have a lot of crust on the outside. But inside? Well I guess I'm plenty soft, because I've been crying over what happened to Tim. Here he was, this young guy coming off an absolutely sensational season, then this sickness hit him. It was devastating. I would have been tickled to see him come to Darlington or any other track and run one lap, just to show he could come back and drive a race car. To have him come here and do this is mind-boggling. . . . It's just wonderful. Rick Hendrick and Tim agreed that if Tim could do it here he could still do it anywhere. Mark my words, after what I saw today, there's no doubt. Tim can still do it."

The next day, which was April Fool's Day, Hyde called Parsons and talked about how fast Richmond had run. Parsons, who was 45 years old, had crashed hard in the race that had been held at Darlington on that Sunday, two days before Richmond's test. Parsons was already beginning to think about how much longer he could be competitive in Winston Cup, and the fact that Richmond had run so much faster than he'd been able to run in qualifying did nothing to ease those doubts. But Hyde left out one important piece of information in his conversation with Parsons.

More than a decade later, Johnson and Parsons were sitting in Johnson's office one day reminiscing about Richmond.

"I told Benny that Tim had four left-side tires on that day. He said, 'What?' I said, 'You didn't know that?' He said, 'Son of a gun.'" Until that moment, Parsons had never known that Richmond's fast times at Darlington that day weren't completely legitimate.

The same day that Hyde called Parsons, Richmond held a press conference at the team's shop in Harrisburg. He said he would make his return on May 17 in The Winston, an all-star, non-points race featuring the 20 most recent race winners on the Cup circuit. After Darrell Waltrip won the inaugural all-star race at Charlotte in 1985, Bill Elliott won at Atlanta on Mother's Day in 1986 in front of a sparse crowd. The event would return to Charlotte Motor Speedway for 1987 and has been held there every year since. Beyond that, Hendrick said, he would let Richmond make his own schedule while continuing to run Parsons for a full schedule the rest of the season.

Richmond went for another "secret" test at Rockingham on April 20, but Higgins and Waid again slipped into the press box and watched the whole thing, with track public relations man Herman Hickman sneaking them soft drinks and snack crackers for lunch. Richmond ran a total of 127 laps on the 1.017-mile track. On May 11, at an open session at Charlotte Motor Speedway, he ran 171.701 mph, more than two mph better than his own track record for a lap and faster than anybody else had gone in the practice sessions. It pleased Richmond particularly that he'd gone faster than Earnhardt, who Richmond had been needling through the press whenever he could. Earnhardt had run 170.723 mph in his test the previous week.

Richmond seemed worried only about how his neck muscles would hold up against the strain put on them by G-forces drivers feel as they speed through the high-banked turns on a track like Charlotte. His neck had bothered him some at the Rockingham test where he hadn't covered as much distance as he'd have to in The Winston, which was scheduled for 135 laps, or 202.5 miles, in segments of 75, 30 and 10 laps. He planned to wear a strap attached to his helmet to give his neck support, and joked that "the only exercise my neck has gotten during the layoff is turning my head back and forth in Florida all spring watching the bikinis go by."

On Friday, May 14, the day before qualifying for the all-star race, Richmond sounded like a man who just wanted to get back to work. "No, I don't have AIDS," he stated. "And, no, I don't do drugs. . . . Entertaining the people in the stands, the fans, is a turn-on for me. And from all the cards and letters I've received from them, they've indicated they enjoy the way I do it. I'm not coming back to lose. I miss hearing the fans call my name."

It was Earnhardt's name, however, they were calling after The Winston, although several of his competitors were actually calling Earnhardt names following one of the most controversial events in NASCAR history—one that featured Earnhardt running through the fronstretch infield grass after contact with Bill Elliott but still keeping the lead in the famously misnamed "Pass in the Grass." Richmond was merely a footnote to all of the hoo-hah afterward, but he finished third and immediately turned his focus forward to his first full race of the season.

Nobody was surprised when Richmond announced the comeback would be at Pocono. He'd won three times and finished in the top five six times in his previous seven starts at the track where he'd made his NASCAR Cup debut in 1980. He also was coming off a 1986 sweep that included the miraculous win after running in reverse for half a lap the previous July.

But if July 1986 was a miracle, what word was left to describe June 14, 1987?

"I didn't see the checkered flag," Richmond would say late that afternoon. "I dreamed about seeing it during my layoff, but I couldn't see it because I had tears in my eyes."

Richmond won the Miller 500. After missing 11 races, after needing a blood transfusion on the morning of the race to bolster his strength for his first 500-mile run since nearly dying in the hospital less than six months earlier, Richmond had won for the eighth time in his past 18 races.

He'd started third and had stayed in contention early, but on a restart on lap 94 he bent the rods between the shifter and the transmission as he jammed the car into gear. That left Richmond with only high gear and forced him to come in for a pit stop, costing him a lap. After his crew pushed him to get the No. 25 going again, Richmond ran down race leader Elliott and got back on the lead lap. When Parsons hit the wall on lap 121, Richmond got the caution he needed to come get the problem fixed well enough so he could continue.

From lap 154 until a late caution, Richmond was leading with Earnhardt up his tailpipe in second. Earnhardt thought Richmond was abusing his tires and was waiting to pounce, but on lap 193 Earnhardt ran through debris in Turn 1 that was bringing out the 10th yellow flag in the race. Richmond stayed on the track, so Earnhardt did too, instead of pitting to see if he'd cut a tire. When the green flew again on lap 196, Earnhardt's tire started going down and he had to hold on to the car over the final laps. He faded to fifth.

Richmond, meanwhile, was gone. The tears started flowing before he took the white flag and never stopped.

"I'd get composed, and then Dale and Bill and Kyle (Petty) and the other guys would drive alongside me to congratulate me and I'd start bawling again," Richmond said. He took an extra lap after the finish so he wouldn't be crying when he got to victory lane. It didn't work. When the climbed out of the car, with a crowd of 90,000 cheering, his mother ran up to embrace him. By that time, any hint of composure was gone.

Hyde was wiping away tears, too. He'd been in racing 41 years, he said, but he'd never had a day like this one.

Neither had Jimmy Johnson. "I have never, ever, ever, ever been around anything that was that gratifying," Johnson said. "I said in the moment when Jeff Gordon won the first Brickyard 400 that it was better than Tim's win at Pocono, but as soon as I said that I said, 'No, it wasn't.' Nothing will ever top Tim coming back at Pocono and winning that race."

A week later, at Riverside—the 13th race of the 1987 season for the rest of the field—Richmond showed that Pocono had been no fluke. He won again, passing Phil Parsons—Benny's brother—for the lead late in the race and pulling away from there. He won by a comfortable two seconds over Ricky Rudd. It was Father's Day, and Richmond dedicated his 13th career NASCAR Cup victory to Al Richmond.

Richmond had won the past three points races he'd entered, and nine of the past 19. He was still saying that he felt only 80 percent back, but after finishing fourth at Michigan the team announced he planned to expand his '87 schedule to include eight more races following the Firecracker 400, all on superspeedways. He'd skip Bristol, Richmond, Dover, Martinsville, North Wilkesboro and Rockingham because "I don't want to overdo it and jeopardize going for the championship in 1988."

It was, almost, as if Richmond believed it was no longer a lie to say that he didn't have AIDS and was dying.

"I think Tim was in denial and so was Mother," Welsh said. "He thought he was going to beat it. He wasn't going to give up. I think he knew he was dying, but there's a part of you that won't admit it. Part of you knows it and part of you doesn't. So you go on with the façade that you can beat it and you're going to be around."

But the part that was trying to hold up that façade, however, was beginning to lose its grip.

"At Riverside, Shav Glick wanted to talk to Tim," Chip Williams said. Glick is the longtime motorsports writer for the *Los Angeles Times*, one of the most trusted and well-liked members of the racing media. "I went down and asked Tim about it and Tim said, 'I'm not talking to him. I can't trust that SOB.' I said 'Shav? You have to be kidding?' But he wouldn't do it."

Williams went to his boss at NASCAR, Les Richter, and Richter said to let it go.

"We went to Daytona the next week and we were supposed to get head shots of the drivers in these different caps with all of the sponsors," Williams said. "I got a photographer and he was going to get Tim after practice. I sent the guy down there and he came back and said he wasn't going to do it. He asked, 'Is this for Chip Williams? I am not doing it.'

"I went to talk to him and asked what the problem was. He said, 'I'm not doing anything for you.' I walked off. I was steaming. Later, he walked up to me in the garage and just lit into me. I lit back and we were yelling at each other. Darrell Waltrip tried to break us up and we both turned around at the same time and said, 'Screw you!' Darrell walked off. We argued for 30 minutes and finally Dick Beatty made us break it up. The whole thing was the paranoia. Shav Glick was out to get him and then I was. You knew something was up."

Richmond qualified 23rd and finished 22nd at Daytona, but there was one more happy day to come. On July 18, Richmond ran 155.979 mph in qualifying to set a track record and win the pole at Pocono, where he'd go for his fourth straight victory at the track where so many wonderful things had happened in his career. It was his 14th career pole. Richmond led 13 laps early, but his engine lost power and he parked on lap 120, finishing 29th.

He started 16th at Talladega the next week, and finished 11th.

The fairy-tale comeback story was losing its momentum—and heading for a very unhappy ending.

C H A P T E R   16

Time is elastic. Every hour is always 60 minutes, but spend one tossing and turning through a sleepless night, and it seems like a lifetime. At dinner with friends though, where the food is delicious and the conversation is lively, an hour goes by in the blink of an eye.

In August 1986, Richmond was the toast of Watkins Glen. He won the first NASCAR race there in years and took part in a memorable celebration later that night at the Seneca Lodge, reviving tradition by having one of his tires hung on the bar's wall alongside the withered floral wreaths presented to past Grand Prix champions there. A local archer, in keeping with another tradition originally begun to celebrate bow-hunters who'd bagged a deer, drilled an arrow through Richmond's cap into the wall.

But just one year later, when Richmond left Watkins Glen, the arrows were being shot directly at him.

There had been three races since Richmond's back-to-back 1987 comeback wins at Pocono and Riverside. Chip Williams had seen changes in Richmond, and he was not the only one. Richmond's clothes weren't quite as neat, his hair imperfectly coiffed. He'd gained back the weight he lost while battling pneumonia, and perhaps a little more.

"Before I got sick," Richmond said in a *Sports Illustrated* article, "I cared too much about what people thought of me. Now my goal is to enjoy Tim Richmond as Tim Richmond."

After his victory at Pocono, Richmond said in an interview with the *St. Petersburg Times*, he suddenly felt depression sweep over him. "What am I going to have to do to enjoy myself?" Richmond thought. "I'd been thinking, 'What if we'd been able to start at the beginning of the season and run every race, if my season had started out like it did, except at the beginning? Where would I be?'"

Richmond remembered being in his hospital bed thinking about what he could do to make a living if he never got well enough to race again. "I went to St. Bart's on vacation," Richmond said. "They had jet skis and windsurfers and this guy was sitting there under an umbrella in his lawn chair renting these things, just taking the money in—taking in that and everything else on the beach. I thought that would be fine. Then I thought about being a gardener. I began thinking about how much life meant to me and the almighty buck wasn't the only thing. I was going to sit back and enjoy it. Either that or pack my bags and get on my Harley-Davidson and go. Maybe buy a sport-fishing boat and charter it or just go to fishing tournaments.

"But now that I'm back, I don't have a boat, don't have a lawn chair, don't have nothing."

Nothing, he insisted, but a new definition of happiness. "Up until the point I got sick, I was never very content," Richmond said. "I was always more concerned or nervous about getting past the next step down the road, achieving the next success. I wanted to be at the top of the ladder, and I wasn't enjoying any of the rungs along the way to the top. . . . I was miserable for 10 years because I wasn't a champion, I hadn't won that many races. My mind was always clicking, trying to figure out what to do next to get further down the road, instead of stopping and enjoying what was taking place. I've been given a chance to appreciate things a whole lot more now. You don't know how much you miss something until it's gone."

And then, with a smile, Richmond added, "But I don't miss pneumonia."

Richmond also had clearly missed the people and the pace of life on the road, and others were beginning to notice that he seemed to be trying to make up for lost time.

He'd become friends with singer Huey Lewis—at a concert in Kansas City, Richmond fell off a runway leading to the stage where Lewis was performing. Some thought Richmond was drunk, but Richmond said he just fell on his "weak ankles."

Lewis was in upstate New York with Richmond in August 1987, hanging out at The Glen as an "honorary crew member"—and trying to keep up with Richmond off the track. Tom Higgins saw Richmond at a restaurant on Saturday night. "He was obviously very intoxicated," Higgins said. "Hey, I was a drinker, too, and I knew how I felt the next day when I'd been out too late at night. I was worried about him."

It was rainy on Sunday morning. Two hours before the scheduled start of every NASCAR Winston Cup race, a meeting is held for the drivers and crew chiefs entered that day. Rules and procedures are reviewed and any questions the drivers might have are answered. Attendance is required—if a driver or crew chief misses the meeting, that team's car starts at the rear of the field.

"Everybody was in the room and the meeting had already started," Williams said. "Tim came in through a door on the garage entrance side of the building, where it looks like you'd be coming into the back of the room. But the way it's set up, it was the front of the room. He comes in and his eyes are all bloodshot and his hair was a mess. He was standing where everybody in the room looked right at him, right behind Dick Beatty. His eyes were darting around everywhere."

As the meeting broke up, Williams said, someone asked Richmond if he was OK.

"He made another one of those 'Why are you out to get me?' comments," Williams said.

Actually, some were. As soon as the meeting was over, the talk began. Within a few minutes, a cabal of drivers had formed and gone to NASCAR officials with an ultimatum. "There was pretty much a mutiny on him," said Barry Dodson, at the meeting as Rusty Wallace's crew chief. "He'd been to a bar downtown there and was there about all night. He was just having fun and partying. It wasn't time to race. When it was time to race he went and raced. But some of the people who were well respected in the sport went to NASCAR and said, 'If he's going to race, then I'm not.'"

Higgins heard the same story. "Four or five of the top stars told Dick Beatty that NASCAR had a choice—if he runs the race, we don't," he said. "NASCAR got a tremendous break when it rained the race out."

NASCAR officials weren't of a mind to let the drivers tell them how to run the race, but they also were concerned about what they saw. Before it became clear the rain would force the race to be postponed until the next day, they considered "suggesting" to Hyde that he find a reason to pull the car off the track after just a few laps. But the rain kept that decision from having to be made.

By Monday, the mood had changed with the weather. Richmond looked much better. He started fourth and finished 10th without incident. But the doubts, the suspicions, the fears sparked by all of the rumors—and at least a dash of long-held envy at the things, real or imagined, Richmond had been able to get away with over the years—were all coming home to roost.

"A lot of people point to that Watkins Glen drivers' meeting and him showing up hung over or whatever and say that was the smoking gun that meant it was over for Tim," Kyle Petty said. "But was he hung over, or was it some medicine he was taking or had he been up all night because he was sick? That's the point. Everybody initially thought he was just drunk. How many times have drivers showed up sick for drivers' meetings? At Sears Point (in 2004), I had food poisoning and was up all night long. I could barely hold my head up, and anybody could have looked at me sitting in the corner and said, 'He must have been out all night.' People just assumed that out of Tim.

"Watkins Glen was the big deal that got everybody talking. I don't even remember seeing him at that meeting, but I've heard that story 10 million times. I think people were looking for something. There are three sides to every story, mine, yours and the truth, but that was almost the point when that story started it spread like wildfire. Who was feeding that fire? Did the people who wanted him out finally get their piece of evidence? I've talked to people who swear they were there that day and there's no way they were there. But they latched their wagon onto that and said, 'This is what we need to put him away forever.'"

It took just one more race for Richmond to run out of second chances.

At Michigan, Richmond's Chevrolet had been good in practice before qualifying. When it came time for him to make his run, the car was on the line but its driver was not there. A frantic search began, and someone finally discovered that Richmond was asleep in his motor home.

"He had the coach locked and they went around and looked in the window," Jimmy Johnson said. "He was laying there in the bed asleep and they beat on the window to get him up. They finally did get him in the golf cart. He said, 'Wait a minute, I have to put my t-shirt on.' He was superstitious about it. But he was so out of it he tried to put the t-shirt over the top of his uniform."

Richmond was also pulling on his shoes as he rode along in the golf cart, asking no one in particular, "Where are we?"

Johnson and Hyde climbed on top of the team's hauler to watch Richmond's qualifying lap. "We could hear the car, but we couldn't see him," Johnson said. "He never got it up on the banking and still was 25th fastest. He pulled in and jumped out and ran to the bus. Tim was standing at the coffee pot shoveling down coffee. Les Richter was looking for us and he was hot. I was on the phone to Rick telling him what was going on. He told me to do what I could and we'd have a meeting on Monday."

Later, as the garage was closing, Johnson was leaving for the day. He thought Richmond was already in the bus.

"I headed out and in the middle of the garage Les Richter and Dick Beatty were standing there," Johnson said. "They crooked their finger and said, 'We need to talk.' They said, 'What in the heck is going on with your driver?' I was trying to stall them and say he wasn't feeling well or the car wasn't right. Out of nowhere, Tim was just standing there. To this day, I have no idea where he came from.

"All of the inspectors were waiting to have their final meeting of the day before going home. Tim said to Richter, 'You're talking about me, aren't you?' Richter said, 'Of course we are. You show up drunk for the drivers' meeting at Watkins Glen and the drivers are complaining about you. What are you going to do to fix it?'

"Tim was turning red and Dick Beatty was trying to calm him down. Tim said, 'Let me tell you something, I am sick and tired of officials talking about me and saying things that are not true.'

"Beatty said, 'Tim, I want you to look over there and point out any official who has been saying things about you. I will fire him tonight.'

"Tim said, 'Junior.'

"Beatty said, 'Who? We don't have an inspector named Junior.'

"Tim said, 'Bill France Jr.!'" referring to NASCAR's president.

"I grabbed Tim by the waist and drug him out of the garage," Johnson said. "I called Rick and said, 'We have a serious problem.'"

Hendrick knew Johnson was right, but he still believes there may have been more to what was going on than what seemed obvious. "I think people were getting medication confused with drugs," Hendrick said. "They thought Tim was on drugs or drinking or both. He was trying to do what he needed to do. And Tim was so good, the other drivers all wanted him out of there. They'd do what they could do to get him out."

Richmond was taking AZT, which Dr. David Dodson said was just about the only treatment AIDS patients in 1987 had on their side in what was still a losing battle.

"Most people didn't really know what was wrong with Tim, but they suspected a lot of things," Dr. Jerry Punch said. "Those who suspected he had a drug addiction thought that because he would have bursts of energy followed by hours of fatigue. That might have been the throes of some of the illnesses related to HIV. For you or me, when we're tired our candle might flicker and flicker, but it will still burn for hours. In that situation, he would fall off the shelf and just have to go lay down. So he'd disappear and be late for things."

That Sunday at Michigan, August 16, he showed up late for the driver's meeting again. When the race began, it was clear that things were not right.

"Tim got very anxious on the radio," Johnson said. "You could tell in his voice something was wrong. He was not Tim. He came into the pit one time and they handed him a cup of water. He just sort of poured it down the front of his face and chest. You could tell something was wrong. On the radio he was saying, 'Harry! Harry! Something's wrong! Harry!' It was like an anxiety attack."

Richmond blew his engine and would finish 29th.

"He came off Turn 4 trailing smoke," Johnson said. "He never said a word, just drove into the garage. We were in the pits and took off as fast as we could. He parked the car between the garage and the coaches and by the time we got there he was running to his coach. I will never forget, Dennis Connor walked over and punched that tell-tale button on the tachometer." The button flicked a lever to the point at which the engine had blown. It went all the way around, indicating Richmond had mashed in his clutch and revved the engine until it blew. "It was pegged. He couldn't stand it any longer."

Richmond had not planned to enter the August 22 race at Bristol, and the following weekend was open on the schedule. He was entered in the Southern 500 at Darlington on September 6, where he would have been the defending champion. But on September 3, before qualifying, Hendrick announced that Richmond's entry had been withdrawn. The team said the driver was once again under a doctor's care. Reporters called the Cleveland Clinic but there was no Tim Richmond registered.

There was, however, a Lee Warner.

A few days after the Southern 500, Higgins learned that Ken Schrader had been hired to drive for Hendrick Motorsports for the 1988 season. He figured that meant Schrader would go into the No. 25 car. A day after he confirmed that Schrader indeed did have a deal, the team issued a statement saying Richmond was "retiring for the near future."

A month later, *Charlotte Observer* columnist Tom Sorensen traveled to Ashland and spent two days interviewing and interacting with Richmond. It remains, Sorensen said, one of the most memorable experiences of his career as a sportswriter.

Tooling around town in Al's Cadillac, Richmond gave the grand tour of his hometown. He pointed out a yard where he once landed a helicopter to impress the woman living there. Sadly her husband, whom Richmond hadn't known about, was home at the time.

Richmond brushed off the drug and AIDS rumors once again, revealing to Sorensen that he'd voluntarily taken two drug tests, one in late 1985 and another on August 28, two weeks after the Michigan race. The first test had come back negative. He said he hadn't heard about the second.

Three days after that second test, he'd gone back to the Cleveland Clinic for a check-up. He hadn't been in for months. Doctors advised him not to race and wanted to admit him. He resisted, but Evelyn Richmond put her foot down. Richmond was in the hospital five days, meaning he was there the day he was withdrawn from the race at Darlington. He then went to Ashland, where he'd been except for a day trip he'd made to New York City the day before Sorensen arrived—to get a haircut.

Richmond talked about returning to Indy Cars, about running for office, about becoming an actor and, once again, about renting jet skis on St. Bart's. He talked about buying a big yacht and sailing around the world or traveling around the country giving pony rides to children.

Richmond took Sorensen to Club 42, an Ashland roadhouse where Richmond had been a regular. Sorensen was trying hard to keep up, but at one point decided he needed a cup of coffee to brace himself. "If you drink another cup of coffee," Richmond said, "this interview is over."

Al Richmond showed up with a friend, and when Tim saw his father he flashed in anger at the thought that he was being checked up on. Tim confronted Al and when the friend intervened, there was a brief shoving match. The next day, though, all was forgiven. At times, Sorensen found Richmond at ease. At times, though, he was on edge. Startled by the click of a photographer's camera, he jumped up from a recliner and yelled, "What's that? Did you hear that?" He thought he heard a similar click on a phone call, too, and responded similarly.

When Sorensen went to the airport to return to Charlotte, he upgraded himself to a first-class ticket. He didn't really care what the expense account ramifications might be at his newspaper. "I had to do it, it was the only way I was going to be able to get on that plane and get home," he said. "Those two days just wore me out."

It was as though Richmond was trying to cram the rest of the life he still had to live into what life he feared he had left.

"I almost died," Richmond told Sorensen. "I had a bad illness. I came back and whipped their butts. I retired. It's like I'm writing a book, except that instead of writing it, I'm living it. What can I live now for the next chapter?"

CHAPTER 17

One day before Dale Earnhardt was honored as the 1987 NASCAR Winston Cup champion, NASCAR president Bill France Jr. conducted his annual press conference at the Waldorf-Astoria Hotel in Manhattan. It had become part of the year-end festivities for France to deliver a "state of the sport" speech and deal with reporters' questions.

On this occasion, he had a surprise announcement. France had apparently finished his remarks and was leaving the stage. Abruptly, he stopped and walked back to the podium.

"I have mixed emotions about this, and before I say anything I'm going to tell you I won't take any questions," France said. "We are going to inaugurate a compulsory drug-testing program next season."

Details of the program were still being worked out, France said. But in light of the incidents of the previous season that led to Richmond's departure from the sport, the first question on everyone's mind was obvious.

"I know what people are going to think," Dale Earnhardt told Tom Higgins immediately following France's announcement. "Their first impulse—Tim Richmond, because of all the rumors that have surrounded him. . . . That's unfair. I never saw Tim do a thing with drugs and I don't know anybody in racing who did, either. But if we'd had this earlier, maybe Tim wouldn't have had to go through all of that grief."

What Earnhardt didn't know in December was just how much grief was still to come.

When Richmond won the pole for the July race at Pocono in 1987, he became eligible to compete in the Busch Clash, a special non-points event for drivers who'd won poles the previous year that helped kick off Speedweeks at Daytona International Speedway the following January.

One of Richmond's problems, however, was that he didn't have a car to drive. Rick Hendrick had hired Ken Schrader to drive the No. 25 Chevrolets for 1988 after Richmond had "retired" the previous season. Given all that had happened, the incidents at Watkins Glen and Michigan and all the rumors that were still swirling, Hendrick said there was no way he could have put Richmond in one of his cars for the Clash or the Daytona 500 the following weekend in 1988.

"NASCAR was still trying to rule the sport with such an iron fist," Hendrick said. "Back in those days you just didn't say anything or do anything to cross NASCAR.

"I don't think they were ready for a guy like Tim, but I don't think Tim bothered them in the beginning. . . . We didn't have a problem with them until the Watkins Glen thing, though. That's when the wheels started to come off. We just had to get him out of the car and get him healthier. There was too much talk going on.

"He didn't want to come clean with what was wrong with him. I think he was embarrassed. . . . People could see that he wasn't well and they thought the worst, that he was strung out on drugs.

Tim and his folks didn't want to level with people. We were in a Catch-22. We had sponsors and we had to go on and tell him to get right and then come back. I knew that he was what prompted the drug policy. I really didn't blame NASCAR. It was something that needed to be done. Tim probably brought it on a little bit earlier than it would have been. If he had been a guy not winning races, it would have gone right under the radar and not made any difference. He was so high profile and at the top of his game, and he was a magnet for attention and he craved it. He was a guy they couldn't control.

"We couldn't put him in a car for 1988. I didn't want to see him get hurt, and he just didn't need to do it."

Richmond called Tim Brewer, who was working for Junior Johnson. Brewer said he asked his car owner if there was anything the team could do for Richmond. "Junior said, 'He's too hot to touch right now,'" Brewer said.

Richmond was determined to run one more race, however. He bought a new, all-white driver's uniform with a helmet to match. On January 20, a few days before France and NASCAR were to unveil the details of their drug-testing plan during the annual preseason media tour hosted by Charlotte Motor Speedway, Richmond appeared on an ESPN television show and declared he was ready to race.

"Come Daytona time, I am going to put my money up to secure a NASCAR competitor's license," he said. "I'll take the physical and, if I get the license, then everyone will know I am ready to come back."

Richmond had stopped taking AZT weeks earlier. "He was suspicious (NASCAR) was going to try to do something to frame him," said Dr. David Dodson. "He came in to see me and had a drug test done. He wanted to be sure that he was clean and that the AIDS medication would not show up."

Richmond went to NASCAR's headquarters in Daytona Beach for a closed-door meeting with officials on January 26, and came out declaring, "as far as I'm concerned I have no problem with NASCAR and NASCAR has no problem with me."

On Thursday, February 4, even though he still had not secured a car to drive, Richmond participated in the draw for a starting position among the 13 drivers qualified for the Clash. He drew the 12th spot, ahead of only Harry Gant, with Geoff Bodine and Earnhardt on the front row for what would be the first event in which carburetor restrictor plates would be used to slow cars at Daytona and Talladega. The previous year, Bobby Allison's car had gone airborne at nearly 200 mph and nearly flown into the stands at Talladega.

Following the draw for starting positions, Richmond was taken to produce a urine sample to be submitted to testing for drugs. He was the only driver asked to submit such a sample.

Richmond spent much of the day Friday trying to finalize a deal with car owner Ken Ragan to drive Ragan's Ford Thunderbird in the Clash. But on Saturday morning, NASCAR announced that Richmond had failed his drug test.

"He (Richmond) was tested and submitted a urine sample Thursday," NASCAR said in a statement announcing that Richmond had been suspended indefinitely. "It was tested by NASCAR Drug Advisor Dr. Forest S. Tennant Friday. Richmond was informed of the indefinite suspension by NASCAR officials Saturday morning. NASCAR's Substance Abuse Policy, first announced publicly on January 25, requires an immediate suspension for a competitor testing true positive for substance abuse. Suspensions may be lifted at a later date if the competitor tests negative." NASCAR did not announce what substances had been found.

Richmond heard of the suspension from Les Richter around 9:30 a.m. and met with officials before leaving the track around noon. That day, cars entered in the Daytona 500 were making their first qualifying runs. Schrader, driving for Richmond's former team, ran 193.823 mph and won the pole.

"I hate this has happened, I hate it for Tim," Earnhardt said. "He's a good driver. You'd think he would have had his act together before he came down here."

"I'm glad NASCAR did what it did," Richard Petty said. "This proves there was something there. The testing did what it was supposed to do."

Perhaps that's precisely what it did.

NASCAR's drug policy stated that a driver could be reinstated after submitting a clean urine sample, but in announcing the suspension on Saturday morning the sanctioning body had all but assured Richmond would not be able to participate in the Clash the next day. Richmond immediately asked for a retest and, on Saturday night, submitted a second sample at a hospital located just a few blocks from the race track. Given that the next day was Sunday, it would be at least Monday before the second sample could be sent to Tennant's facility in California for testing and the results could be determined.

Richmond, remember, had been tested by his own doctor and knew that sample had been clean. The answer to the question Earnhardt had asked when he heard about the positive result NASCAR announced was, perhaps, that Richmond did have his act together. After submitting the second sample Saturday, Richmond taped an interview for the CBS telecast of the Clash. He told Ken Squier that not only had he not taken drugs in 1988, he had not done so in his career.

"I'll bet anything NASCAR wishes it hadn't taken the test," Richmond said. "Now they can't let me on the track. If I went out there and hurt someone . . . I understand their position. I just maintain that I've made mistakes and you've made mistakes. There has been a mistake made on this drug test, somehow or other. I am not guilty."

A day later—and a day too late for Richmond to try to keep Earnhardt from winning the Clash—NASCAR agreed. On Monday, Richmond was reinstated. The test on the second sample, the one Richmond had provided Saturday night, came back negative.

Chip Williams found himself in a tough spot, trying to explain how one sample could be positive and one supplied two days later could be negative. "There was no mistake on either test," he insisted.

Higgins was covering the whole mess for *The Charlotte Observer* and was already getting weary of the story. Speedweeks, under ideal circumstances, are a grind for reporters covering the events as extensively as Higgins's newspaper did. In 1988, it was getting ridiculous.

"It was the most bizarre thing I went through, I imagine, in my whole career," Higgins said. "They kept us at the track, I know one night until midnight, waiting on test results to be flown in from California. It was maddening. You're at the track all day and you sit around waiting for the tests to come back, then they come up and say they didn't get here. One time they announced Federal Express couldn't get it there, I said, 'My God, with the time they've had, the Pony Express could get it here!' It was beyond weird."

The weirdness was only beginning.

In reinstating Richmond, NASCAR added a stipulation to the physical examination he would still be required to take before being cleared to drive in the Daytona 500. Dr. Ronald Hinebaugh, the track physician at Daytona International Speedway, wanted a release from Dr. Dodson and also said he needed to see the medical records showing how Richmond had been treated for the pneumonia that had been reported as the illness that had sidelined him.

Richmond was still talking to Ragan, now about driving Ragan's Ford in the Daytona 500. To make the field for that race, Richmond still had several options. If he practiced in at least one session by Wednesday, he could start in one of the following day's two 125-mile qualifying races and, if he finished high enough, earn a slot in the 500 field. Or, if he didn't get things worked out by Thursday, he could buy the ride in a car that had made the race and, provided he got in at least one practice, race on Sunday.

Richmond also was lining up some powerful allies on his side. He contacted New York-based attorney Barry Slotnick, who had defended New York subway gunman Bernard Goetz in criminal court. "I was in New Orleans when he called me and said he needed me in Daytona," Slotnick said. "I was in New Orleans to speak to a group of about 1,500 people, but he said he would do whatever it took to get me down there. He said he could fly me to Daytona and then have me back the same day. He had me picked up the next morning in a private plane and I spent most of Tuesday there."

Slotnick came in firing heavy guns.

"There is no reason why he should not be driving this Sunday unless bureaucratic red tape holds him back," he said. "Tim's position is he's not going to be intimidated by anybody." Richmond was not going to turn over his medical records to Dr. Hinebaugh. "As a matter of principle, we will not allow NASCAR to treat him in a discriminatory way." But Richmond would allow his doctor at the Cleveland Clinic to submit a written report on the treatment he'd received for pneumonia in late 1986. That was not enough for NASCAR.

The clock was still running. On Wednesday, *The Charlotte Observer* reported that Slotnick had told the newspaper that the substance NASCAR would say it found in Richmond's drug tests was pseudophedrine—the active ingredient found in the over-the-counter cold medicine Sudafed. But by Thursday morning,

Richmond had not been cleared to practice and therefore was not entered in the 125-mile qualifying races.

That afternoon, Williams was in the press box at the Daytona track when France called him.

"He said, 'You need to come over here,'" Williams said. "After the 125s I went over to his office and he said, 'We've got a problem.'"

France wrote down two words—pseudophedrine and ibuprofen. "You know what those are?" France asked.

"I said, 'Sudafed and Advil?'" Williams said. "He said yes, but in large amounts. We got on the phone with Tennant and the lawyers and started writing a statement. We wrote it three or four times and I finally took it up to the press box to read it to the reporters. It was a lonely feeling—I knew it was going to be bad. I went down to the front of the press box and I said, 'Here's what we've got.' I read the statement and then started to take questions. The first guy to ask a question was (veteran reporter) Dick Mittman, and he was flat-out mad, I could tell. He said, 'You threw this guy out because he had a bad cold and a headache?' And it started from there. They beat us up pretty bad, yelling that we'd ruined this guy's career."

The statement Williams read said tests on the sample Richmond had submitted a week earlier, on Thursday, February 4, had shown "five to 20 times the normal" dosage. "As defined in . . . the NASCAR substance abuse policy, the misuse of a legal prescription drug or over-the-counter drug is strictly prohibited." Tennant concluded, Williams told the reporters, that Richmond "could not have safely driven a passenger car with the amount of pseudophedrine that showed in his system."

Two years later, in February 1990, Tennant ended a four-year stint as adviser to the National Football League's program after a series of published and broadcast reports questioned the credibility of his work. One report, aired on a television station in Washington, D.C., cited two former employees of Tennant's company saying that Tennant had falsified the positive report in Richmond's case, with one saying they had been told that NASCAR suspected Richmond of using drugs and wanted to "do something about this guy."

Citing sealed court documents it obtained, the report said Tennant had told NASCAR that Richmond's first test was positive for opiates and amphetamines. But one employee said Richmond's first test came back negative, and then Tennant ordered that it be run a second time. That report also came back negative, the employee said. Tennant then sent the sample through additional, more sophisticated screening and found the over-the-counter medications. But the report said that the additional testing would not have determined any quantity of the medications still in Richmond's system.

Tennant denied falsifying any reports, saying the sources of the stories criticizing him were disgruntled former employees looking to take revenge.

By the time that all came out, however, it was far too late.

In the 72 hours before the 1988 Daytona 500, Richmond and his closest friends were beginning to realize that NASCAR had a roadblock across every possible avenue Richmond tried to take to run in one more race, something he badly wanted to do.

"He was hyped and ready to go," Welsh said. "Mom didn't want him to do it, but he wanted one more time."

Richmond's hotel room at Daytona Beach became like a "war room" as he tried to get around the obstacles being piled in his path.

On Saturday, the day before the 500, Slotnick was back in Daytona at a news conference with Richmond at the hotel. "Events of the past 10 days reflect on an effort to besmirch and defame my client," the attorney said. "The unsuccessful charade began with a campaign of rumors and innuendo directed against Tim. There was a concerted effort to defame Mr. Richmond."

Slotnick delivered a letter from Dr. Dodson to NASCAR on Saturday morning, stating that Richmond was in good health and was not nor ever had been a drug abuser. But Dr. Hinebaugh, the track doctor, said he still needed to contact Dr. Dodson to confirm the information. At that time, the final practice before the Daytona 500 was already underway.

The clock had run out.

"Tim and I were up in his room with a bunch of people that Saturday," Fred Miller said. "He had on a shirt that had 'Sudafed' with a red circle around it and a line across it, like it said, 'No Sudafed.' We were laughing about NASCAR screwing up."

Richmond was determined to get the last laugh. He had arranged to hire a plane to pull a banner across the track during the 500 on the following day. His original intent was to have the message be a profane jab at NASCAR, but some of his friends talked him out of that. Instead, during a race that Bill Elliott won for the second time in three years, a plane flew over the 2.5-mile track and its massive grandstands trailing a simple message—one that would turn out to be a sad goodbye.

"Fans," it read, "I miss you—Tim Richmond."

By whatever means, NASCAR had won its battle to keep Richmond off the track at Daytona. From the distance provided by more than 15 years, it's easy to be critical of the methods used in doing so—singling out Richmond for drug testing, the questionable nature of the testing itself and the stalling tactics employed in demanding to see medical records for Richmond that no other driver returning from an injury or illness had ever been asked to provide.

As is always the case, however, it's important to consider the context on both sides of the issue. Rumors that Richmond had

AIDS were abundant before he'd left the sport. Rumors that he was using drugs had been around for far longer. Even without having proof of either case being true, if NASCAR placed any validity in those rumors at all, its officials had to consider what might have happened had Richmond been involved in a serious crash in which he or other drivers had been injured. Would it have been right to expect emergency workers to tend to Richmond after a crash without having protection against potential exposure to the blood-borne HIV? Such precautions in emergency response situations would eventually become standard procedure, but were not yet at that point in early 1988.

If the first drug test sample Richmond provided was mishandled, what if NASCAR did not know that and simply was reacting based on what it was told, that Richmond had tested positive? Frankly, NASCAR never expected there to be a positive test. Its officials figured that any driver who used banned substances would decline to take the test and therefore not get a license. Even when the second sample was clean, NASCAR was in a tough spot. Had Richmond been allowed to race and then been in a crash in which others were hurt, could the other drivers involved not then turn around and sue NASCAR for letting a driver who had a positive drug test on get back into the car?

All of these questions lingered as the circuit left Daytona and headed into the 1988 season.

Richmond's bid to come back for one last hurrah was over. It was time for him to fight another battle, another one he wasn't going to win.

CHAPTER 18

After being shut out of SpeedWeeks, Richmond stayed around Daytona for Bike Week, an annual gathering of motorcycle enthusiasts that coincides with motorcycle racing at Daytona International Speedway. Richmond and Bob Jones, an old friend, spent the week taking photos around town and put them together in a hardback book called *Run to the Sun.*

Richmond had packed the driver's suit and helmet he'd bought to use in the Busch Clash or Daytona 500 in a bag and brought it back to the condominium near Fort Lauderdale when the debacle there was finally over. It sat on the table, ready to be picked up and taken to the next track, for months.

"I didn't know what to do for Tim," Rick Hendrick said. "I told him, 'You really just need to get well. You're fighting a losing battle with NASCAR, forget about all that stuff and do whatever you can to live as long as you can.' You can't beat the system, and even if he did by hook or crook, he couldn't have beat it physically. If they'd told him to go race he couldn't have done it, physically.

"He was bitter at the world for what happened to him and bitter at them. Here was a guy who went from living his dream and having the world in his pocket to waking up one morning and the world was coming to an end for him. I think he was hurt and bitter due to the disease he had. I think anybody would be. There were all of the accusations against him. It was just a shame for his fans and for his family."

In April, Richmond sued NASCAR and five of its officials for $20 million—$15 in compensatory damages and $5 million in punitive damages—alleging his career had been ruined because they wrongly labeled him a drug abuser. It was the rebel's final act of defiance to a sport that he felt had turned its collective back on him.

There was, in early May, a brief flutter in the rumor mill that Richmond might try one more comeback in the 1988 running of The Winston all-star race. He'd won two races in 1987, so he was eligible, and Hoss Ellington said he'd be willing to let Richmond drive one of his cars, but much of that speculation seemed to be coming from Charlotte, where the speedway was trying to sell tickets.

NASCAR still insisted that it would have to see Richmond's medical records before he would be cleared to race, and Richmond's attorneys said he would not supply them.

By late that year, pretrial activities surrounding Richmond's lawsuit against NASCAR and its officials began. NASCAR asked a federal judge hearing the case in Charlotte to order Richmond to come to North Carolina to be examined by a physician. It subpoenaed his tax returns, records of every blood or urine test he'd taken since 1980 and records of each time he'd visited a doctor, psychologist or counselor. Richmond did come to Charlotte in October to give his deposition, but the interview was postponed shortly after it began when Richmond could do little more than give his name and address without getting confused.

On his best days that year, Richmond had been calling some of his friends and asking to see them. Bob Tezak, for instance, heard from his old friend in February before the Daytona debacle.

"Tim called me up and asked me if I was coming to Daytona," Tezak said. "I told him I wasn't sure. He told me he needed me to come because he needed to talk to me, and he sounded like he was serious and it was important. So I told him I would be there. I went to Daytona and we got checked in and everything and I went to Tim's room. He told me to sit down, and he explained the whole thing to me. I was in total shock. We talked about what we'd done and how good we both felt about it, about how far he came from 1980 until 1986."

Richmond gave Tezak a copy of a poster that had become popular among the driver's fans. During his hot streak in 1986, and after the Hayride 500 he'd taken part in, The *Charlotte Observer* staged a photo shoot of Richmond, dressed in one of his expensive suits, standing in front of several bales of straw at the speedway in Charlotte. When the photographer was ready, and with a fire hose standing by, the bales of straw were set on fire. Richmond was photographed standing amid the flames, and after a few frames were taken the fire was quickly extinguished. The photo ran in the newspaper and was turned into a poster that became a hot commodity.

"I have that on my wall," Tezak said. "On the poster it says, 'To Bob: Thanks for the career.—Tim.'"

Richmond also called Raymond Beadle.

"He wanted to know if he could come to the ranch in Texas," Beadle said. "He came out there and told me he had AIDS. He wanted to see his friends one last time."

He had those frank discussions with only a few of his other friends. With others, Richmond either talked around the subject of his illness or never made contact at all. Barry Dodson talked to Richmond for the last time at Daytona in February of 1988. The last

time Jimmy Johnson saw Richmond was when the driver was running away from the car toward his motor coach at Michigan on the
day of his final NASCAR Winston Cup race.

On December 29, a judge in Charlotte ordered the Cleveland
Clinic to release Richmond's hospital records. Three weeks later,
less than a month before the trial was to open on February 6, the
case was settled. Terms were not released, and the matter was
dropped.

Richmond was through fighting.

From the middle of 1988 on, Richmond had some days when he
had enough energy and spirit to get out. But as the months passed,
they became more rare and the bad days became far too common.

"He really became a recluse," Sandy Welsh said. "He didn't
come out of his bedroom. He was hurt to the core. The spirit and
the fire, with the disease and everything, that did it. That broke it.
It was like he gave up. The sooner this is over, the better. He stayed
in his room and kept his blinds closed. He was in the condo in
Florida and it had a beautiful view of the water, but no. It was
always dark and the drapes were drawn. He wouldn't turn the television on. He just laid there in that bed."

In early 1989, Richmond had one of his good days and was out
with some friends messing around with a motorcycle that they
couldn't get started. They decided to tow it behind a car to see if it
would start while rolling, and Richmond climbed on. When the
car pulled forward, the clutch on the motorcycle popped and
Richmond was thrown onto the pavement. He banged his head and
suffered cuts and abrasions, which had potentially serious conse-
quences since infection was a severe risk because of the presence
of AIDS. He was in the hospital for several weeks after that accident, eventually being transferred to Good Samaritan in West Palm
Beach. He was released briefly, but by early May he had been
admitted again.

Evelyn Richmond, who had spent her entire life doting on her only son, was constantly by his side. Al had sold the family business in 1988 and moved to North Carolina and then to Florida to help his wife and son cope with Tim's declining condition.

As the bitter reality set in, Evelyn simply could not bring herself to deal directly with the inevitable. Tim didn't want to talk about it with Evelyn, either.

Sandy Welsh became their go between.

"Mother knew Tim wasn't going to get better, but they still wouldn't admit that to each other," Welsh said. "At one point, she called me and said, 'Sandy, you've got to talk to Tim.' Whenever Tim wanted Mom to know something that was really an issue for him, he'd say, 'Sandy, you have to talk to Mom, and this is what I want you to tell her.'"

One day, Evelyn began a conversation Welsh will never be able to forget.

"Sandy, I have to know this," Evelyn began. "But I can't ask Tim this."

Evelyn wanted to have Tim cremated so she could keep his ashes with her.

"I can't ask him that, I can't let him know that I know he's going to die," she said to Welsh.

"Mom," Welsh said. "Tim knows that."

Evelyn insisted that only Welsh could ask the question.

"I went to see him in the hospital," Welsh said. "We were talking about it and he said, 'No, I do not want to be cremated, and I do not want to be put in the ground.' So I told Mother that. She sent me out to a mausoleum in Ashland. I bought the spots. And we didn't discuss that any more."

On Sunday, July 23, ESPN showed its tribute to Richmond during its broadcast of a race from Pocono. Evelyn was there in the hospital room, as she was every day. There were times when

Richmond was lucid and carried on conversations with her. There were times when he spoke but made no sense. And there were times he was unable to speak at all.

"One time we thought that he was dying and Mom called me to come down there," said Welsh, who'd also moved to North Carolina and bought a house in the same neighborhood where Tim lived. "I got on an airplane and had to change planes and I called. He had been unconscious. I told Mom to put the phone up to his ear, because I wanted to tell him that I loved him. She did it, and I said, 'Tim, I love you.' And he said, 'I love you.'"

Evelyn's vigil was relentless. She stayed as late as the hospital would allow her to every night and was back by eight the next morning. There was a nurse watching Richmond closely during the hours when Evelyn had to get some rest. Evelyn was not feeling well, and hadn't been for months, but Al and Sandy thought that was understandable given the ordeal she and her beloved son were going through.

Dr. Dodson said that Richmond's condition was steadily deteriorating. The family had hired guards to stand by the door to make sure nobody could get in to see Richmond, who didn't want anyone to see him in the shape he was in.

"Finally, Tim just didn't want anything else done," Dr. Dodson said.

On the morning of August 13, the phone in Evelyn's condo rang. It was just after 4 a.m.

Evelyn answered. It was Tim.

"Mom, I want you to come over here," he said.

Evelyn shook the cobwebs of sleep from her mind.

"What is it, Tim?" she asked. "It's four in the morning."

Tim was insistent.

"I want you to come over here," he said. "I want to talk to you."

Richmond's nurse took the phone and spoke to Evelyn.

"By the time you get over here, he'll be asleep again," the nurse said. "Just wait and come in the morning."

Evelyn hung up.

Barely an hour later, at 5:12 a.m., Tim died.

"Mom never forgave herself for not going to the hospital and being there when he died," Welsh said.

That day, the NASCAR Winston Cup circuit was racing at Watkins Glen. Rusty Wallace, driving for Blue Max Racing, won the race and, at Barry Dodson's behest, dedicated the victory to Richmond who'd been in that very same victory lane at the zenith of his career just three years earlier. But nobody in the NASCAR world—or outside of Richmond's family—knew that Richmond had passed away.

Welsh traveled to Ashland and went to a funeral home where a family friend was working. She picked out a coffin because she knew Evelyn would never be able to handle that task. The friend told Welsh he had been expecting her call.

"He said, 'You would not believe the number of calls I've had in the past couple of years, when people didn't know where Tim was, reporters would call to ask if the funeral arrangements had been made already," Welsh said. "They had heard he was dead. It wasn't out what he had, but people were surmising it."

With its ranks still closed, the family was determined to keep the media away and say goodbye to Tim privately.

On Monday, August 14, a caller who refused to identify himself called *NASCAR Winston Cup Scene's* headquarters in Charlotte. He spoke to Deb Williams, the weekly newspaper's managing editor, and asked if she knew that Richmond had died at 5:12 a.m. that day in Good Samaritan Hospital. The caller, apparently reading from the death certificate, listed the causes of death as cardiopulmonary arrest, gastrointestinal hemorrhaging and acquired immune deficiency syndrome.

By Tuesday, reporters were calling every funeral home and cemetery in the Ashland area to find out what they could about the arrangements. They got very little information. Welsh was dealing with Denbow-Primm Funeral Home and had purchased vaults in a mausoleum at Ashland County Memorial Park, which sits alongside Ohio Highway 250 that runs into the heart of Richmond's hometown.

Richmond's body was taken to a funeral home in West Palm Beach where, because he had AIDS, special measures were taken in preparing it for interment. It was then sent to Ashland.

On Tuesday afternoon, Dr. David Dodson confirmed to the media that Richmond had died two days earlier. He declined to give a cause of death or discuss Richmond's medical condition, as the family had requested.

Fred Miller was in Chicago for a business meeting. He'd left drag racing when Raymond Beadle retired and was working with Action Performance, a company dealing in racing merchandise such as die-cast cars and apparel. "I was staying in a Holiday Inn and I picked up the newspaper," he said. "There it was. That's how I found out Tim was gone."

The family's private funeral service was held on Wednesday. "There was media all over town that day, wanting to take pictures of the hearse and all of that," Welsh said. "But we went a back way to the cemetery. It was Mom, Al and I. That's all. My own children weren't even there."

Dr. Jerry Punch, who'd been in touch with Richmond and his family up until the very end, understood. "They'd been through so much, they felt like they deserved a few private moments with him," he said.

The racing community said goodbye on Thursday in a memorial service at Charlotte Motor Speedway. There was no casket, only a helmet on a podium, a helmet Richmond had on the day he won at Pocono in 1983. About 200 people were there.

"There's a hole burning in me right now," Barry Dodson said at the service. "I didn't get to tell him goodbye. There are a lot of people who wanted to tell him how much we loved him."

The media didn't stop digging, and by early the next week it became clear it was not a matter of whether the true cause of Richmond's death would be made public, only a question of when. On Tuesday, August 22, ESPN reported that it had obtained a copy of Richmond's death certificate and that he had died of complications from AIDS.

Al and Evelyn Richmond decided to end the speculation once and for all.

"It was like, Tim's gone, they can't hurt him anymore," Welsh said. "My folks said, 'They can bash us all they want to. Tim's gone now, and they can't hurt him any more.'"

The next day, Dr. Dodson held a news conference and announced that he believed Richmond had contracted AIDS through heterosexual contact. "That's what he told me, and I believe him," Dr. Dodson said. "He absolutely did not use intravenous drugs. He hated needles. He did not get it through a blood transfusion and he did not engage in homosexual activity. The bottom line is if Tim can get this, then anybody can."

The *Charlotte Observer* ran a piece of Richmond's death certificate in the newspaper on August 24. Barry Dodson said that was the first time he actually believed that his friend had been infected with AIDS.

Dr. Dodson said the family wanted the whole story of what Richmond had to be told so that women he'd had sexual relations with before being diagnosed could realize they might be at risk. Men who were part of the sport, some of whom had been with some of the same women who'd been involved with Richmond, also found themselves worrying if they'd been infected.

"They were running helter-skelter when it came out that Tim had that, being tested," Welsh said. "We heard about that."

Tragically, there were women with whom Richmond had had sexual relations who were later diagnosed with AIDS. Some died, and their deaths were every bit as tragic as Richmond's had been. Some women who were with Richmond and who were diagnosed with AIDS are still alive, and the physical and emotional pain they've endured is something only they can truly understand. But someone also gave AIDS to Richmond, and there's no evidence that the person who did that did it intentionally—no more evidence than there is that Richmond ever intentionally spread the virus himself.

Richmond was not an AIDS victim who happened to be a race car driver. He was a race car driver, and a damn good one, who died of AIDS.

"He had it all," Humpy Wheeler said, "and he lost it all."

Perhaps Harry Hyde, the crusty old crew chief who at first had butted heads with the young hot-shot driver who Rick Hendrick had dropped in his lap, put it best.

"You've got a pile of iron sitting there—pipes, sheet metal and rails, stuff like that," Hyde said. "You put it together and one day it turns out to be a beautiful car. You've worked your fanny off on it and you develop a love for that car. . . . When a driver gets in it and does such a hell of a job, you develop love for that driver, too, because you haven't done anything until that driver gets in the car and does the job for you. So I loved Tim.

"I hope he's at peace."

CHAPTER 19

Harold Elliott remembers a day in the North Carolina mountains.

"Tim and I spent the whole day up there," Elliott said. "We stopped in Boone and ate, and then we came down the road. We were going to drive through Taylorsville, and Tim wanted to stop at Harry Gant's house. He loved Harry, but I told him I wasn't going to stop."

The two did stop at a gas station and convenience store in Gant's hometown.

"There was this 1961 Chevrolet sitting out back, and Tim and I thought it was the coolest car we'd ever seen," Elliott said. "We paid the guy $1,200 for it and the next week he put it on a flat bed truck and brought it over to the Blue Max shop. We went out there and looked at it, and then we looked at each other.

"Tim reached in his pocket and gave somebody a $5 bill to go to the store and buy a six-pack of beer. In the daylight, that car didn't look nearly as good as it did to us that night when we had a few beers in us."

Elliott had at first decided it'd be too hard for him to talk about his friend that he still misses to this day. But one morning he heard a song on the radio by country star Tim McGraw called "Live Like You Were Dying." Every time Elliott hears that song, he thinks of Richmond.

"When he came to the track in the morning, he wanted you to be happy," Elliott said. "At the end of the day when he left, he wanted you to be happy. How good was the car running? That wasn't it. Driving the car didn't mean everything; neither did winning races or having a lot of money. One night we were driving back from a race in Richmond. Evelyn was driving the motor home and Tim and I were sitting in the back. We had ended up second behind Earnhardt and I was mad about it. Tim wasn't. He said, 'Harold, you know something? There are 600 million people in China who've never even heard of this sport.' Life was what mattered to Tim. He just wanted to make people happy."

There are days when Barry Dodson is still bitter about what happened to Richmond, and still a little angry that he never got to say goodbye to his friend.

"The part that pisses me off is that they took a human being's life away from him," Dodson said. "Racing was the life Tim knew, it was the life he loved because he knew he was the best. But they took that life before he was dead, and it was sad."

When Rusty Wallace won the 1989 NASCAR Winston Cup championship, Dodson borrowed the sequin-studded tuxedo Richmond had worn to the awards banquet in 1986 and put it on as he accepted accolades as the champion crew chief.

What would he have said to Richmond if he'd had the chance to talk to him one last time? "We would have talked about the good times," Dodson said. "I would have tried to make him realize he was going to a better place. I think he would have wanted to talk about the funny stuff and the accomplishments. We would have talked about the things he was right about and NASCAR was wrong and he showed them. I was right, that's what he would have said. When I go in the track these days and see the motor home lot full, I just smile."

Dodson also smiles when he remembers a day of testing at Charlotte Motor Speedway.

"My little boy, Trey, had to wear leg braces when he was little," Dodson said. "Trey loved Tim, just loved him. One day at Charlotte, we were testing and we'd been out there all day. It was five o'clock, and it had been a hot, miserably sweaty day. But Tim said he wanted to give Trey a ride. Trey crawled in there with his tape recorder and taped the lap and it was as much as I'd ever seen him smile. Tim was running and he wasn't six inches off the wall. I said, 'Pull it in!' I was scared to death and Trey was just cackling. Tim was smiling like that was a bigger accomplishment to him than being the fastest car over there all day long."

Fred Miller thinks about the 40th birthday party Richmond threw for him, after Richmond had first been diagnosed with AIDS but before the disease had finally gotten the upper hand. "He had this '59 Cadillac convertible and we rode around in that," Miller said. "He always had the cool toys. He died way too soon, and he was so far ahead of his time. If you had a Tim Richmond in NASCAR today, you'd have so much money. He had the good looks; he could drive better than any of them. Hell, he could even have his own cooking show."

Geoffrey Bodine remembers a day at the track in North Wilkesboro.

"Back then you just drove to the track and pulled your cars and trucks in there and parked until you were ready to go home," Bodine said. "We both had Chevys that we were driving. It was raining and we were just killing time. The radio in the car he had didn't work. He got in my car and we thought he was just sitting in there to get out of the rain. But my wife and I were on the way home and turned the radio on and it didn't work. Tim had told us that his radio didn't work. She got so mad. When we got home she called him and raised hell. 'Tomorrow, you put that radio back in our car!' she said."

Tim Brewer remembers a day at Pocono when a young driver named Davey Allison, Bobby Allison's son, came over and asked if he could follow Richmond around the track for a couple of laps to learn how to go around the oddly shaped track. "Tim said sure," Brewer said. "Then he went through the tunnel turn and Davey nearly busted his butt. Bobby came over there and said, 'Tim, what the hell are you doing with Davey? Don't you ever take my kid through that turn like that no more.' Tim said, 'Bobby, that's the only way I know how to go through there. They don't give directions.'"

Kyle Petty believes that Richmond's death together with the end of the wide-open 1980s marked a major turning point in the maturation process of stock car racing.

"The sport started to change," Petty said. "It went into the transition where you had major companies, Fortune 500 companies like Coca-Cola and like that come in. We all had to straighten up. Go back and look at the sport over the past 55 years it has been in existence, and the 1980s have to be our college years. All of a sudden, after Tim's death, it was time to go on and make your living and grow up."

As a racer, Petty believes, Richmond had the kind of ability seen only ever so often.

"I may make a lot of enemies saying this, but I am not so sure Dale Earnhardt would have dominated the sport the way he did if Richmond had been around," Petty said. "Richmond had more talent in his little finger than a lot of us ever had, period. It was raw talent, all it needed to be was harnessed and honed. If it had played out that way through the early 90s, would Jeff Gordon have gotten a ride with Hendrick? Richmond would have been that star.

"Go back through the sport's history and certain people jump out in their eras, and Tim was the guy who should have jumped out from our era. Earnhardt carried a lot of it, and by God he could, but he had to carry it a little longer until Jeff was ready. I think we skipped one period in the sport when we lost Tim."

Rick Hendrick first saw Jeff Gordon drive a race car in a NASCAR Busch Series race at Atlanta Motor Speedway in early 1992. He had gone under the track in a tunnel that came out near the foot of the frontstretch grandstands in the track's former configuration and was walking toward the track's suites to meet some friends. As Hendrick walked, he noticed a driver who was smoking his tires as he went into the turns. When he got to the suite he told his friends to get ready because that car was getting ready to wreck. It didn't—Gordon won the race. It reminded Hendrick of seeing Richmond drive the car as hard as it could possibly be driven, and by the end of that year Gordon was driving a No. 24 Chevrolet for Hendrick Motorsports. In 1995, he brought Hendrick his first NASCAR Winston Cup title and, in Hendrick's mind, fulfilled part of Richmond's destiny.

"No question Tim would have won championships," Hendrick said. "If he had stayed healthy, him and Harry Hyde together? I don't know how much they would have won. We were getting smarter. Gary Nelson was helping us get smarter. With Tim's ability and Harry's stability, we would have just gotten better.

"And what people don't realize about Tim is that as he started winning he started to change his focus. He started getting ready to be a champion. He was maturing, but the disease and getting sick is what unraveled everything."

Tim Richmond wore the No. 13 when he played high school football at Miami Military Academy. He won his first NASCAR Winston Cup race on June 13, 1982. He finished his career with 13 victories. He died on August 13, 1989. And on November 13, 2004, more than 15 years after his death, he was inducted into the National Motorsports Press Association's Stock Car Racing Hall of Fame in Darlington, S.C. Harry Hyde and Humpy Wheeler were inducted in the same class.

When NASCAR celebrated its 50th anniversary during the 1999 season, a panel of experts selected the 50 greatest drivers in the sport's history. When Richmond made the list, some people in the sport were surprised, not because he didn't belong on the list—clearly, he did—but because it had seemed at times that in the decade since his death the sport was trying its hardest to pretend he'd never existed.

Evelyn Richmond defended her son's memory as long as she had breath in her body. Sandy Welsh believes now that the fatigue and weakness her mother showed in the final days of Tim's life were also signs that Evelyn had cancer. Until Tim was gone, however, Evelyn had no time to worry about her own health. Once Tim had died, she had no will to worry about it, either.

Evelyn died on November 28, 1994.

"Mom grieved herself to death," Welsh said. "When he was sick she never left him for three years. After he was gone, she went with him. When Tim was sick she wouldn't go to the doctor. Afterward, she was diagnosed with depression and actually her cancer was in an advanced stage and there wasn't anything they could do. They never found the source of it, when they found it her liver was just consumed in it and it was in her bones. After they diagnosed it, she lasted about three months. That's about what they said it would be.

"She told me, 'I don't want to leave you guys, but I want to see Tim.' And when she died, it was like she was so peaceful laying there. It was like 30 years disappeared. You could just see the difference. It was incredible. I am assuming she saw him."

After Tim's death, Evelyn gave a few of his things away. She gave Barry Dodson the driver's suit Tim had bought for Daytona in

1988, and Dodson has since loaned it to the North Carolina Auto Racing Hall of Fame for display. For the most part, though, Tim's house on Lake Norman remained much the same as it had when Tim lived there.

"The closet still had clothes in it and his cowboy hats and boots on their racks," Welsh said. "Everything in the house, pictures and all, were left the way they were. When Mom died, I went in and started cleaning out her cosmetics and nightgowns and all of that, and Al came to me and said, 'Don't touch another thing.' His theory was that as long as it stayed that way, it was like Mom and Tim were off racing and they would be back."

Al Richmond stayed in North Carolina, where he'd occasionally drop by one of the shops of the race teams where people he'd met in the sport still worked. The racers were always happy to see him, but they said Al never seemed to feel at home when he came around.

He died on November 23, 2001.

Al was interred in the mausoleum near Ashland alongside of Evelyn. He rests on the right side of his wife. Tim is on his mother's left side. Beside Tim is Kimberly Welsh, Sandy's daughter. She died of cancer in 1999.

Welsh sold Tim's house in early 2004. Since Al's death, she'd been going into the house whenever she felt up to it, going through a lifetime of things Evelyn had lovingly collected. "I am a pretty tough old bird, but you can only emotionally deal with that so many days at a time," Welsh said.

Today, much of what she finally cleaned out of the house is in several storage warehouses in Mooresville. The dress uniform Tim wore when he graduated from Miami Military Academy lies on a table, zipped up in a garment bag and stacked along with perhaps a dozen driver's uniforms Richmond wore throughout his career. There are dozens of scrapbooks, some with photos taken by the family from as far back as Tim's days showing horses, others filled with pictures from his racing career sent in by fans when he was alive and after his death.

In one box, there are drawings from Tim's days in grade school—a Rachel Field poem copied in Tim's cursive handwriting mounted on a page with a drawing he did—and his Vacation Bible School graduation certificate from 1961, when he was six years old. Other boxes are filled with magazines and newspapers that include stories about or interviews with Richmond. Several trophies, from his racing career as well as elaborate saddles he won in 4H horse shows, share space with boxes of his cowboy boots and hats.

One of the boxes contains letters sent to Evelyn and Al in the days, the months and the years after their son's death. Some came from family and friends, others came from race fans who'd met Tim only once—or never at all—yet felt compelled to write and share their feelings with his family. Many were addressed only "Al and Evelyn Richmond, Ashland, Ohio," and were still delivered.

"I remember the first time I met him and had the pleasure to talk briefly, back at Darlington in 1986," one fan wrote. "What a thrill for me to stand face to face and talk to the man who made my heart race (faster than any race car). . . . After all those years of imagining what it would be like to talk to Tim it came about, and it turned out to be a greater joy than I had imagined. He was just so nice and I was so clumsy and speechless. I remember thinking that I didn't want it to end, I wanted that to last forever.

"I saw him twice after that, once at Charlotte and then in Bristol after the race, and he remembered me! Each time we talked only briefly, but it still made me happy just to be near him and talk those few moments. Those memories will stay with me for life.

". . . Tim was a beautiful person and I cared for him very much. The hoopla the press has with trying to scorn him and berate all that he was and stood for is a disgrace. I'm really, really sorry you and the family had to deal with such unfeeling and uncivilized individuals.

". . . From time to time I pull out the old VCR tapes of Tim and watch them. When I see that beautiful smile it always makes me cry. But I had the pleasure of knowing him, and the memories of him will stay in my heart. I'm thankful I had the opportunity to meet him and know him in my lifetime. You and Mr. Richmond had a lot to be proud of. Tim Richmond was one of a kind. There will never be another like him."

Another letter contained a picture of a baby boy. "We wanted to send you a picture of our son, Timmy, who is named after your son. I felt that your son was the best thing to hit NASCAR in the '80s. Since I love racing, I wanted to name my son after a driver. . . . If it wasn't for your son's untimely death, I think he would have been the all-time reigning champ. . . . I feel this is the one tribute I can pay to him."

Jimmy Johnson has his own way of keeping Richmond's memory alive.

Every year, when he gets a new calendar, he opens it to the page for August. In the space for August 13, he writes "Tim Died 5:12A '89".

"It's the first thing I do," Johnson said.

"I don't want to forget him."

Celebrate the Heroes of Auto Racing
in These Other Releases from Sports Publishing!